THE REVIVAL OF INTEREST
IN THE DREAM

The Revival of Interest in the Dream

A CRITICAL STUDY OF POST-FREUDIAN PSYCHOANALYTIC CONTRIBUTIONS

WITH AN ARTICLE ON THE 'SPOKEN WORD'

ROBERT FLIESS, M.D.

INTERNATIONAL UNIVERSITIES PRESS, INC.
New York   *New York*

MANUFACTURED IN THE UNITED STATES OF AMERICA

FOREWORD

A SUBSTANTIAL PORTION of this monograph has appeared in *The Yearbook of Psychoanalysis,* Volumes VI and VII. When friends suggested that the review published there be extended and put under separate cover, and the publisher joined them, I eventually agreed because I felt that a path ought to be cut for the students of psychoanalysis through the literature overgrowing *The Interpretation of Dreams.* I owe thanks particularly to Drs. Bertram D. Lewin and Sandor Lorand for encouraging me to elaborate upon an originally short presentation opening a panel symposium on dreams; and to Dr. Lorand, as the copyright owner, for the permission to use the two articles in the *Yearbook.*

To the many authors whose work is the better part and object of this review I am grateful. Since both they and I are attempting to pursue the truth, I am confident that they will, when we disagree, recognize but their own critical attitude duplicated in mine. Criticizing a work thoroughly is a sign of respect; and it is of the worth-while work that Lessing has said its critic should not be lenient. There is but one condition that I would impose upon the critic claiming common cause with the author: *he must document his opinion.* In the present instance the documentation is frequently apt to take the form of a reference to or an abstract from *The Interpretation of Dreams,* or the writings supplementary to it by Freud. If I defend his word I do so merely because it is the record of his observations. These are penetrating and extensive to the extent that the student is often better assisted by reference than by circumlocution; they are, furthermore, fundamental.

What Freud has observed must be learned in order to be augmented, and what he has abstracted must be understood in order to be revised. The first of these propositions implies mastery of technique, the second of theory; falling short of fulfilling one, one cannot either validate Freud's observations or add new ones; falling short of the other, one cannot either place what one sees or improve upon certain ordering principles so as to place it better. Since as many contributions as space permitted are reviewed here, the reader will find examples of different degrees of assimilation of theory and technique. In the case of some of them, concerned with controversial questions, the reviewer is forced to supply opinion; in the case of others he need only supply or explain references from Freud.

Such is not exegesis. The theory of the dream is not only, as its author believed, incomplete; it contains, I believe, even a number of errors. It is in want of addenda as well as of emendations. In the case of one addendum, supplementing the theory of dream speech, the literature contained only a brief report. This made it necessary to investigate instead of reviewing and to contribute toward the problem.

If the student, closing this small volume, feels that besides having been acquainted with some new ideas and stimulated to clarify old ones, he has had a practical lesson in the reading of *The Interpretation of Dreams,* my purpose is virtually achieved.

R. F.

CONTENTS

INTRODUCTION

FREUD'S COMPLAINT, expressed almost two decades ago, of the lack of interest in the dream among analysts is well known: he accused us in the first of his *New Introductory Lectures* of behaving as though we "had nothing more to say about the dream" and "as though the whole subject of dream theory were finished and done with." And he documented his dissatisfaction with the gradual diminution and eventual disappearance of the steady column which the old *Internationale Zeitschrift für Psychoanalyse* had devoted for many years to a "wealth of contributions on various points of the theory of the dream." It is obvious that he speaks of the dream as a subject, not a tool, for psychoanalytic investigation: dream analyses, such as are found in almost every clinical paper, drawing upon but not adding to the theory of the dream, are not pertinent to the content of his remark.

The present review, in re-examining the situation two decades later, shall retain a critical standpoint, survey the bulk of the psychoanalytic literature on the subject, and attempt a brief presentation of what has been achieved. If the volume of work appears small, it should be remembered that Freud's own work has been nowhere more exhaustive than in the field of the dream. If the addenda seem modest, it should be borne in mind that the mastery of the subject, prerequisite to enlarging upon it, is attainable only by a restricted number of theoreticians. And finally, if the contributions are found to be inhomogeneous, this should be credited to the fact that the "predilection for the fragmentary treatment of a subject," to which Freud once confessed, is a necessary characteristic of the psychoanalytic student. His attention, arrested here or there in the course of his clinical work, becomes focused and allows him to abstract from his observation only in order to place his abstraction in a context, fragmentary and inhomogeneous in itself.

Part One

MISCELLANEOUS CLINICAL OBSERVATIONS

This section, continuing, as it were, the defunct column "Zur Traumdeutung," mentioned above, assembles a number of diverse clinical contributions.

I. "DREAM SYMBOLISM"[1]

A Query to Freud

HERBERT WOTTE, a German analyst, reports in the Internationale Zeitschrift für Psychoanalyse (XVII, 1931), under the title *Ein erlebtes Stück Traumsymbolik (A Piece of Dream Symbolism Experienced)* on a dream, "representing the symbolically concealed repetition and continuation of a day-dream immediately preceding it." In this daydream he imagines himself sitting next to an older and very experienced lady, frequently occupying his thoughts. "I would like to touch her breast but her dress is so tight. I slide therefore, sitting to the left of the lady, my right hand towards her back busying myself trying to open the snap buttons on her dress." At this point, the day-

---

[1] The term was retained for the present purpose although it is a misnomer: The symbol (in the psychoanalytic sense of the word), encountered in dreams, is indistinguishable from that encountered elsewhere (e.g., in "association," symbolic actions or works of art). "Dream symbolism" and "symbolism" are synonymous; Freud's remark in the tenth of his *Introductory Lectures*—attenuated but not contradicted in the *Outline*—about a difference between them notwithstanding.

13

dreamer looses track, falls asleep and has the following dream:

> I see myself standing in front of a well-known inn, but not at the front entrance, although I seem to know about its existence because I want to go into the dining room situated directly behind it,—no, I see myself standing before the rear entrance at the rear wall of the house. I am trying to pull the door of the rear entrance open (towards the outside) —but no, it is now a curtain which I penetrate or try to pull aside with great difficulty and effort.

While analyzing his dream, the dreamer recognizes it as the symbolic repetition of the daydream and, in comparing the two, asks himself several questions concerning the choice of the symbol as well as the choice of symbolization. Why an inn (*Wirtshaus*) instead of merely a house? Certain day residues lend themselves to an answer: a particular inn with a front door and a curtain behind it, where he had once bought cigarettes from a waitress and which the dreamer equips with a rear entrance in homology with the lady's blouse. Yet all this information, unsatisfactory as it is in the first place, fails to elucidate what the author considers the main question and which he poses to Freud. "Why (*wozu* = for what purpose) did the dream conceal a latent thought symbolically, after the latter had already been present unconcealed in the daydream?" And Freud answers: because symbolic reflection in the dream *"permitted you an allusion to the person of the mother (inn, waitress) which you could not have achieved while awake.* Your information concerning the age of the lady fits this (interpretation)."

The Symbolism of Losing Teeth

Dreams of losing teeth, to be distinguished, according to Freud, as "dreams upon dental stimulation" (*Zahnreiz-*

träume) from "dreams of the dentist" (*Zahnarztträume*),
are typical dreams only inasmuch as they contain what one
might call a multiple symbolization. Puberty masturbation
(Freud), parturition (Jung, Jones) and the death of a
person close to the dreamer are symbolized in them. The
latter in "parodistic" fashion (Freud) or with the qualification (Abraham) that the loss is not painful since many
others are still alive and will compensate for the loss. If
the tooth, as in dream of the dentist, is pulled by another
person, the idea thus represented is that of castration. The
resistance to analyzing these dreams is reported by Freud
as enormous, and their interpretation has, in his opinion,
remained incomplete.

SANDOR LORAND   (*On the Meaning of Losing Teeth in
Dreams*, Psa. Quart., XVII, 1948) reports on a dream in
which the much overdetermined symbolization appears to
him, in addition, as representative of the wish to be again
the still toothless baby assured of the nursing mother.

H. S. DARLINGTON (*The Tooth-Losing Dream*, Psa. Review, XXIX, 1942) while assembling American Indian
and Mexican folklore, where the dream is understood as
signifying—or, as such folklore has it, prophesying—the
loss (death) of a relative, presents, without making a point
of it, a remarkable quasi-experimental confirmation of this
symbolization. He reports a dream of his own which, instead of elaborating upon the thought of the death of his
parents in terms of the loss of teeth, elaborates upon the
thought of the loss of teeth in terms of the death of his
parents. Suffering pain in two molars on opposite sides of
the jaw and afraid of having to have them extracted, the
author falls asleep and dreams of a railroad yard in which
trains are being shunted in such a manner that first his
mother, and then his father—who in reality had both been

dead for two decades—escape narrowly being crushed to death.

LESLIE H. FARBER of Washington and CHARLES FISHER of New York (*An Experimental Approach to Dream Psychology Through the Use of Hypnosis*, Psa. Quart., XII, 1943) have engaged in an experimental study of symbolism by repeating, in essence, the hypnosis experiments first undertaken by Schrötter of Vienna in 1911 on which Freud reports in his *New Introductory Lectures*: Schrötter ordered his medium to dream of sexual occurrences and found the sexual material replaced in these dreams by well-known symbolizations. The present investigators have, in part, reversed the procedure by telling the medium "symbolic" stories or dreams, and obtaining from him the translation of the symbol. Thus their version of the dentist dream— "A man sitting in a dentist's chair while the dentist tries to pull his tooth. He pulls and pulls. The dreamer is in great pain when the dream ends"—is interpreted by the subject to the extent that the man was having his "vital organ" cut off; while the same dream, told of a woman, was translated as "giving birth to a baby." This example, representative as it is of the core of the study, shows, again, the "experimental approach" as leading, not as the title suggests to the psychology of the dream, but merely to the phenomenon of unconscious employment and unconscious understanding of symbols.[2]

BELA MITTELMANN (*Psychoanalytic Observations on Dreams and Psychosomatic Reactions in Response to Hypnotics and Anesthetics*, Psa. Quart., XIV, 1945) described

[2] The authors' comments upon the *theory* of hypnosis suffer from the same shortcoming as does the bibliography appended to their paper, which omits the fundamental work by Freud (in *Group-Psychology and the Analysis of the Ego*, London, 1922), Ferenczi ("Introjection and Transference," *Psa. Review*, 1916), and Schilder (*Über das Wesen der Hypnose*, Berlin, 1922).

a series of five dreams of a patient under the influence of nitrous oxide administered as an anesthetic during the performance of dental surgery upon five different occasions. Since this patient, a thirty-five-year-old woman artist, was in analysis at the time it became possible to analyze each of these dreams separately and by so doing perhaps influence form and content of the next. The dental surgery is, unfortunately, not specified by the author beyond "drilling"; extraction proper may therefore not have been involved. The stimulation is here, of course, an external one and the "dreams" need not—and do not appear to be —dreams in the sense of the term when it is applied to the mental activity of the sleeper. Yet the unconscious understanding of these "dentist dreams" as revealed in the subject's associations is the ubiquitous one: castration. (Genital injury, onset of menstruation, abortion.) The author's interest and the slant of his contribution are not, however, directed toward the subject of symbolization, but —as indicated by the title—toward psychosomatic reactions to anesthetics. The *"consistent* elements" in these reactions were, as far as the dental patient is concerned, her "struggle against the loss of her faculties of perception and mastery" under the drug; while "the dream content and the concomitant feelings as well as the psychosomatic phenomena—laughter, weeping, and vomiting—*varied* with the different aspects of the unconscious problems with which the patient was struggling."

PAUL FEDERN (*A Dream Under General Anesthesia,* Psa. Quart., XVIII, 1944) has subjected these "constant elements" to an interesting study. The anesthetic is again nitrous oxide, the occasion the extraction of four teeth, yet the dream, analyzed by the author, is his own. Unafraid of employing himself as a subject for analytic investigation, Dr. Federn attempts to separate what he terms "ego contributions to the dream" from the "productions of the dream work." And, in doing so he records a rare experience. It was the first time in his life that he had to undergo general anesthesia and it occurred shortly after his expatriation. This is his own report about anesthetization and dreaming:

I disliked having the lump of gum thrust into my mouth but was reconciled when I felt it was not hard but elastic. At this moment, I had my last thought before the anesthetic took effect, a thought—without any fear—that I might die and that I should use my last moments to consider intensely and philosophically the end of this life and to make an important decision of some sort in regard to accomplishing something in case I should continue to live. Then I felt the strange but rather sweet taste of the gas, a slight dizziness—and I vanished as a personality. There was no disagreeable feeling while inhaling the anesthetic, no respiratory difficulty, no optic disturbance whatever. I fell asleep suddenly, as I had many years ago, and without any feeling of faintness or realization of losing consciousness. Consciousness was lost so quickly I could observe no details.

The dream did not begin immediately after the last conscious thoughts. There was an interval in which my ego lost all its mental charge—its cathexis (*Besetzung*) —and was extinguished. A short time afterward mental life returned. I did not know that I was dreaming; I had not forgotten my antecedent life; I felt myself with my own character and name. However, I lived in completely changed surroundings and I possessed a strength of will power, quickness and certainty of decision, intensity of action, the like of which I have never experienced before, either awake or dreaming.

I was the chief military commander and the chief statesman of great territories, and I put in order one province after the other. In the dream, I knew which country, far in the east, it was. But in remembering I cannot decide whether it was China or Greece. These provinces had straight-lined frontiers like the states of the United States of America. But the country was not America.

The time I seemed to live through while I was strenuously endeavoring to reform all these countries was very long; it appeared to last for half a year. I accomplished my task with continuous strain and tension. Everything was decided in a hurry and carried through quickly. I was very severe with myself but at the same time fully and continuously contented with the way I performed my duties. Never in my life have I felt such happiness or satisfaction with my personality and with my work. It was the strongest "feeling of oneself" and the greatest enjoyment of one's own self one can imagine. The singular events of the dream followed each other with enormous speed, all actions were carried out with perfection, one after the other, and in complete order and very quickly, since it seemed necessary to act as quickly as possible during the whole dream. Life was a glorious and victorious fight without any conceit or show; I distinctly felt that I never failed to follow the motto: Do what you have to do.

Suddenly the glory ceased. One of the surgeons spoke to me. Immediately I tried to remember all the details but was aware of only the skeleton of the dream.

The following are the essential points in the author's interpretation of his dream: "The principle of wish-fulfillment is overt. . . . Instead of obeying the nurses like a well-behaved child, the dream made me a very masculine superman. Thus, I compensated for being fettered and for the loss of manhood and strength which was sustained symbolically, in having a number of teeth taken away."

At the same time: "I must go back to my childhood to find daydreams which correspond to this anesthesia dream. At the age of 10, I remember, I read with enthusiasm a book for boys, which, as I recall it, was named *Liu-Pa-Yu;* it dealt with a Chinese story and I became very interested in the fate of the Chinese and wanted to go to the Orient myself and become Emperor of China. For a long time, I was teased about this.

"The other possibility, that the country dreamed of was Greece, has two sources; at the age of 13 or 14 I deeply resented the defeat of Demosthenes and the victory of the Macedonians over Greece. The second source is more recent. In discussions, I have frequently demonstrated the parallelism between ancient history and recent events; and made the forecast that another European-Asiatic empire might be attempted by the militarily progressive and politically aggressive northern tribe of the Germans. In the dream, I myself was the helper of all these countries."

All in all, however, Dr. Federn concludes that his dream "happened in deepest sleep and not in awakening," and that: "The main, manifest dream events can be traced to stimuli and to changes of the mental state brought about through anesthesia."

The interpreter isolates five different "stimuli" to which the "subject's" mental state reacted with the reported alterations:

(1) "My last conscious thought was that I must consider seriously my future plans. This thought created—like an autosuggestion—my heroic course during the dream," and "produced a dream shaped like Caesar's *veni, vidi, vici.*"

(2) "While the last conscious thought directed the whole dream, a last perception determined the choice of the field in which the dream played—and more especially its form. After my awakening, the straight-lined frontiers remained as a clear visual remembrance. One might think that they are sufficiently explained by the frontiers between the states of the United States. Yet I know that while the characteristics of the map of North America in my dream were provoked, the stimulus occurred before losing consciousness. When I looked to my right side, I saw the illum-

inated and magnified X-ray pictures of my teeth. The pictures were quadrangular, they were hanging side by side, and I thought that they demonstrated which teeth had to be operated on. My last visual interest was given to them. They represented what had to be changed."

(3) "My identification with the surgeon was another, the third, recent source of my dream. What the surgeon did in physical reality, I accompanied with parallel deeds in the world of my dream. This world of my own was not limited, either by judgment or by reality-tests; both are lacking in dreams."

(4) "This identification expressed itself by the use which I made of the fourth stimulus for my dream, the operation itself. In my dream, one province was put in order after the other; and I remember that I hurried from one to the next. Repetition of an element is rather a rare dream phenomenon; usually it corresponds to a repetition of the fact represented by the element; it is probable that each extraction was transformed by the dream-work (i.e., the whole unconscious mental process that builds up the manifest dream out of its latent sources) into one after the other of my separate political and military activities; I also was repairing each ruined country to a sound and good state."

(5) "I pass over some deeper associations and interpretations and may only add as a fifth source of the dream my thought when I decided to have my teeth removed. I intended a full and energetic repair for good; and so I 'repaired' my provinces in my dreams."

The analysis, reported here, does not, however, satisfy the inquisitive author. The "enormous delight" in his dream, the "great speed of the happenings" and the "tremendous strength" of his "ego-feeling" have remained unexplained, because "only the dream-contents were dealt with and not the peculiar personality state during the dream."

He ascribes these phenomena to the personality state and he ascribes the personality state to the anesthetic.

With regard to the strong *ego feeling,* he explains that both "the sudden disappearance of the ego and the intensity of the re-awakened mental ego"—"it was only a *mental* ego," he emphasizes, "with no trace of the *bodily* ego"—were produced by the anesthesia:

"Complete anesthesia allows the dream-ego to become strongly cathected, because no danger exists of being awakened, as there would be if, in normal sleep, the manifest dream exerted too strong a stimulation on the ego, which is feebly cathected and passively exposed. In anesthesia, the dream has lost its function of protecting sleep, since this function has become quite superfluous."

The *speed of the happenings* is attributed to the absence of fatigue and sleepiness by the author, who considers slow-paced dreaming "a symptom of psychosomatic fatigue," and who believes that the "lack of any interference of body-ego, due to the interference of the anesthetic, combined with the enormous intensity of mental experiences and deeds" is responsible for the "extraordinary impression of extension of time."

With regard to the *"personality state":* in anesthesia, "no danger of awakening threatens sleep . . . . no announcement of too strong stimulation compels the dream-ego to withdraw any recathexis, as it does during usual dreaming," . . . it remains a "strongly cathected mental ego," with "its boundaries well guarded against instinctual urges as well as against irrationalities coming from the unconscious." It shows happiness ("happiness is a corollary of ego-cathexis") and "the main qualities of the normal ego, volition, clearness, rationality," thus distinguishing itself from the ego of a dreamer.

The fortuitous choice of the object of this searching investigation and the importance of its results for certain aspects of the theory of the dream as well as of that of the ego compel the reviewer to a few comments, critical with regard to the fundamentals.

In the first place, Federn's interpretation appears to be out of focus. The dream did not, in this reviewer's opinion, "happen in the deepest sleep and not in awakening" but occurred while the subject was waking up; it was, in other words, an "arousal dream." If the arousal stimulus is (as it had been in the present instance) an external one (the voice of the surgeon, equivalent to the proverbial alarm clock), the dreamer never fails to experience it as an interruption of a dream whose analysis shows invariably that the apparent interruption had actually been the stimulation. (If a spontaneous dream is interrupted, the arousal stimulus precipitates an extension of it, after the fashion of the "Dream of the Burning Child.") The dreamer's erroneous conviction is supported by two circumstances, typical for so many arousal dreams: the tremendous distortion of the experience of time and the interpolation of ready-made fantasies *(fertige Phantasieen)* into the dream. (Cf. Freud's analysis of "Maury's dream of the Guillotine"!) Federn's "Caesarean fantasy" is such a one; the "regression through sleep," implying, as it does, a concomitant "historical" regression, causes him to elaborate upon his last conscious thought about his future-American-life by reviving the puberal fantasy about his future life at the age of thirteen: the fantasy of being Caesar. That the ego feeling (may we call it the "feeling of self," *Selbstgefühl* and remember the subjective nature of this phenomenon in contrast to the objective—if hypothetical —nature of the ego?) is a purely mental one, may well be an addition to the phenomenology of such ready-made fantasies in the dream. That the "speed of the happenings" is ascribable to the drug appears possible, yet it requires corroboration.

In the second place, although the author remarks in passing upon "the loss of manhood and strength . . . . sustained symbolically" by the extractions and upon his identification with the surgeon as one of the "recent" sources of his dream, he fails to exhaust the implications of these data; i.e., their relation to each other and their central significance for the analysis of his dream. A *symbolic* "castration" (the term does not occur in the paper) is to the unconscious a *"castration."* The "hypnopompic" realization of his castration is responded to with a dream, denying it through an identification of the castrated dreamer with the castrator, the surgeon. This type of "identification with the aggressor," combining "mastery through transformation into activity" with a compensatory inflation of the narcissistically injured ego, explains the "strongest feeling of oneself" and "the greatest imaginable enjoyment of oneself" reported by Federn, in its economical aspects. It is capable of transforming the "illiterate" immigrant, asking asylum, into the conqueror, who, while invading province by province, forces them to adopt his language, because it changes the patient into the doctor, who "came, saw and vanquished" as consultant, diagnostician and surgeon. Anyone sufficiently familiar with the implications of the castration complex in general and their particular applications to the situation of the physician compelled to turn patient, will require additional evidence for a specific influence of the drug.

II. "TYPICAL" DREAMS

The chapter in *The Interpretation of Dreams* and the extremely fragmentary treatment in it of the subject by

Freud are well known. In recent years several authors have attempted to contribute to this topic.

MARIE BONAPARTE *(A Lion Hunter's Dreams,* Psa. Quart., XVI, 1947) presents a brief casuistic study of two unusual *"examination dreams,"* brought very well into focus. They are dreams of a South African lion hunter, who as a young man was picked up and dragged off by a lion, whom he escaped eventually by climbing a tree after having stabbed the beast fatally with his knife. While recovering from an infected wound, his ordeal had repeated itself, in the hospital, in traumatic dreams, of which the sixty-eight-year-old man was unable to report to the author anything except their occurrence. Yet "for a long time," at the point of the interview, dreams elaborating upon the episode had changed from a repetition of the successfully accomplished feat to an experience of failure. It is of these later dreams that the investigator presents two examples. In one of them his gun fails the hunter, who pulls the trigger in vain, and the shot finally going off, hits the lion without piercing him, while the bullet falls to the ground. In the other he climbs a tree, after failing to shoot at the charging lion, but a huge bull buffalo butts the tree with his head. "The tree sways to and fro and I fall. Then I waken to find it is only a dream, *for which I am terribly thankful."* The author evaluates this as "a kind of hunter's examination," and perceives in the last (italicized) words of the dream report a confirmation of the fact, emphasized in *The Interpretation of Dreams,* that the examination elaborated upon in the sense of failure is always one passed successfully in real life. Freud's solution: a dream reactive to the anticipation of an imminent test in the dreamer's life, misunderstood by the "waking institution" *(wache Instanz)* as far as the consolation expressed by it, is concerned. (You have once before been afraid of failure and have succeeded.) Bonaparte, who suspects that what had begun to be "tested" was the potency of the aging man, adds that the hunter's rescue from his accident was not, as it is in most cases, a passive one, but that he owed his life to his active presence of mind, courage and skill. And she concludes that "this circumstance may have contributed to no small degree to turning the traumatic anxiety into an examination-dream."

SANDOR S. FELDMAN (*Interpretation of a Typical and Stereotyped Dream Met With Only During Psychoanalysis,* Psa. Quart., XIV, 1945) describes and interprets a new "typical" dream. This dream, occurring "only during analysis," depicts the analytic session as "disturbed by others" in the office or in adjoining rooms whose presence robs the patient of the privacy to which he is entitled and provokes his resentment. Associations are difficult to obtain and interpretation, "as does that of all typical . . . . dreams, opens the way to the deepest and most strongly repressed wishes of the patient. A remarkably swift flow of associations ensues . . . . and relief is felt by the patient because a resistance has been overcome." The author describes six different variations: in the first, "the analytic session is disturbed by the presence or movement in and out, of the analyst's wife or some other member of his family"; in the second the disturbers are not the analyst's relatives but the patient's; in the third they are strangers. In the fourth variation, "the dreamer is disturbed by the presence of two analysts," one of whom "usually plays a male role, sometimes as the assistant of the other"; in the fifth "another analyst, of the same or the opposite sex, is substituted for the real one," and in the sixth "the analyst is the same but the office is somewhere else or the furniture is somewhat different or the couch has another location." The deepest unconscious infantile dream wish underlying this typical dream is, in Dr. Feldman's words, the dreamer's wish for the mother, the desire "of being in perfect fusion with her, in a relationship without danger, especially that of castration." The patient's annoyance at the disturbers—relatives, represented either directly or through their opposites: strangers—is, in his opinion, the expression of "a resistance against the emergence of persistent strong desires for these persons." And it is, so the author explains, the projection of these desires upon the analyst that transforms the relatives into his. The last three variants represent, in the author's opinion, likewise, variations upon the theme "love of the mother." Of the two analysts only one analyzes the patient, the other loves him, as will the new analyst whom he had found in his dream. The change in location, layout or equipment of the office "expresses the patient's desire to change his relation to the analyst" in the sense of the relationship between mother and child.

In the only dream transcribed in this study (it belongs to the "third variant") the patient entering the waiting room is disturbed by a couple, husband and wife. Husband and analyst, wife and patient, respectively, pair off; the former for an analytic session and the latter for an amorous walk. Both couples meet again in the waiting room and the patient feels that the analyst resents "any advance toward the woman and that you think I have encroached on your territory." The dream is instructive beyond the dreamer's competitive ("active" oedipal) conflict, mentioned, and his homosexual ("passive" oedipal) problem, omitted in Feldman's interpretation, because it illustrates the capacity of a "typical" dream to absorb other—typical as well as individual—material.

The reviewer, who has for a long time been interested in this dream and considers its monographic treatment a merit, is prompted to a few critical comments based upon his own clinical observations.

(1) It is true, but it is not true without exception, that dreams about the analysis are distinguished by the presence of persons other than the analyst and his patient.

(2) Feldman's six variations are not inclusive enough; there are variants of this dream befitting none of these variations.

(3) The presence of other persons may, but need not, be equivalent to their "intrusion"; dreams, for instance, in which a female patient is affectionately accepted by the analyst as a daughter, or preferred to his wife as a companion, are not too infrequent. The affective experience of the dreamer, in other words, may, but need not, be that of "resentment"; the co-ordination of one particular feeling to all dreams about the analysis is, therefore, without justification.

SANDOR S. FELDMAN (*Interpretation of a Typical Dream: Finding Money,* Psa. Quart., XVII, 1943) reports another dream, and declares it a typical one. Here the dreamer finds money in the ground; first one coin, then many, "not only pennies, but nickels, dimes, quarters," and searches—with pleasurable and mounting excitement as well as with growing concern "that some of the coins have escaped his attention"—for "more and more" of them "almost indefinitely." The author, who cites the occurrence of the dream in a sixty-year-old woman and in a little girl, finds that the "dream-thought expresses the desire that the earth be the source of life only, and not of life and death" (the earth "in which we are all buried after death and from which, according to the well-known legend, we came"). And he explains that it is coins that are found "because coins, unlike bills, are regarded as imperishable and retain something of their value even in the event of devaluation." The anxiety in the dream is traced to the fear of

death; "the dreamer wants to exploit all the pleasure-pos-
sibilities of life." Hence he reassures himself that "he will
find more money some other time, that the sand always
contains money and that it is not necessary to collect all of
it at once."

RUDOLPH M. LOEWENSTEIN (*A Post-traumatic Dream,*
Psa. Quart., XIII, 1949) reports on a dream, typical, although not perhaps in the sense of the "typical dreams."
It is a dream, reproducing a severely traumatic event of
the day before—danger of and rescue from drowning—in
a substantially altered form yet with an equally happy
ending. The analysis supplies the material for the alteration: a similar rescue from fire instead of water in the
dreamer's fourth year of life, nightmares in the course of
his "infantile neurosis," the later identification with a
heroic man who saves himself twice by his own efforts
(once from death of tuberculosis and once from political
execution) and the symbolic metamorphosis of death into
(re-) birth, converting the dreamer about to return to the
womb into a "revenant" from it into life. The author contends that the identical aspects of dream and traumatic
experience follow the repetition compulsion, while divergent elements are conditioned by wish fulfillment.

MILTON W. MILLER (*Ego Functioning in Two Types of
Dreams,* Psa. Quart., XVII, 1948) attempts to establish the
"typical" nature of two other, often observable dreams, by
opposing what he terms "mirror dreams" to what he terms
"catastrophic dreams" and considers their occurrence as
indicative of the relative capacity of the ego to cope with
the "main conflicts." He contends that the dream of looking into a mirror is a "narcissistic image" that "evidences
an attempt by the ego to look at a mobilized conflict." If
this is an interpretation, it is an "anagogic" one, representing an "allegorical" approach to the dream. Of the extreme

limitations inherent in this approach, the author appears
unaware. The *thought:* "I take a look at myself" can, of
course, be translated into pictorial language; such is done
in metaphorical speech as well as in the hallucinatory experience called dreaming. But in both instances thought
remains thought. The translation does not transform it
into a metapsychological process. As for the "catastrophic
dream" where "the anxiety mobilized is overwhelming
and must be avoided by the ego," this reviewer has been
unsuccessful in his attempts to distinguish its description
by Miller from that of the nightmare.

ALFRED GROSS *(Sense of Time in Dreams,* Psa. Quart.,
XVIII, 1949) postulates likewise, although hardly more
convincingly, the existence of two typical categories of
dreams. Both have a certain relation to time: "the first
type refers to time in precise figures of astronomical time;
the second type alludes to time by presenting situations of
frustration through time." The first type is found by the
author to be "a distorted expression of a highly charged
and conflictual *current* object relationship"; while "the
second type is an (often repeated) attempt to reduce a
traumatic ('tragic') frustration *of the past* to a trivial frustration of the present." Three examples are offered. The
first is a patient's dream, dreamed over the week end:

I am sitting in the car at a gasoline station. The man
there should fill the tank. It is twelve-thirty, an hour until he closes. He puts two gallons into the car and then
stops. Instead of going on filling the tank, he climbs into
the car and sits down in the back seat. I sit in the other
back seat and think the man is a homosexual and is going to attack me. I feel very angry.

The author's comment:

The dreamer was in a jumble of adverse feelings
against his wife over the week end, and was looking for-

ward to his analytic hour on Monday. That, however, was in conflict with repressed homosexual undercurrents. It required two sessions of associations, inhibited by resistance, to analyze "twelve-thirty" and "an hour until he closes."

There is, naturally, no doubt that the reference to time in this dream constitutes an allusion to the object of a currently conflictuous relation in the transference. But it is neither shown that the allusion through time is distinguished, in this respect, from any other allusion, nor that the numerical designation is specific. Why could the analyst in the dream not have borne other hallmarks; why could the session not have been alluded to through an indeterminate reference to time, such as "everyday?"

The second example, a recurrent "dream of missing trains" is discussed without reference to either its typicality or its symbolic meaning (= not dying) as established by Freud; while the third example is the "dream of the Wagner performance" from *The Interpretation of Dreams*. This is the dream of a social acquaintance of Freud, used by him merely to illustrate one single phase of the dream work: the transformation of thoughts into pictures. (See the remarks to the preceding contribution reviewed in the present section.) It does, for obvious reasons, not lend itself to a demonstration of the author's thesis. But: does the dream do so at all? Is it ever capable of representing a current transference conflict without simultaneously representing the past conflict that is currently being transferred?

III. DREAMING AND ACTING OUT

RICHARD STERBA (*Dreams and Acting Out,* Psa. Quart., XV, 1946) presents a short clinical communication, characterizable by an amplification of its title to "dreams and their subsequent epitomization through symbolic or symptomatic action in the transference situation." An example:

A woman patient who has arranged to live near the analyst's home in order to continue her treatment over the summer is seen by the author running up the steep path and storming up the stairs to the office for her session. ". . . When I opened the door, she did not take off her coat but rushed into my office, threw her coat on the floor, and flung herself on the couch, completely out of breath. She began immediately to relate a dream from the preceding night, frequently interrupted by attempts to catch her breath. She dreamed that her mother, while talking with her by telephone, had to interrupt her speaking continually" because of dyspnea caused by labor, while "giving birth to a baby." The patient, by being breathless herself and interrupting her own speech, identifies herself with her parturient mother, and in this fashion fulfills a wish "most urgent in her early childhood," and "most important" for the understanding of her disturbance.

The author comments upon the fact that the action preceding the dream report appears as equivalent to an association to the dream, whereas actually both are expressive "of the same unconscious instinctual dynamism which succeeds in breaking through the repressive forces of the ego, particularly when the defences are loosened up through the analytic work." The paper contains good teaching material, because it demonstrates the regressive nature of the analytic situation, which permits the patient to include the analyst in a bit of "repeating," while transferring onto him the role of parental objects.

IV.　THE HYPNOTIC "DREAM"

MARGARET BRENMAN (*Dreams and Hypnosis,* Psa. Quart., XVIII, 1949) deserves an extensive quotation of her basic remarks on the so-called hypnotic "dream."

Since Schrötter's fragmentary, unfinished investigation in 1911 of so-called "hypnotic dreams," she writes with refreshing directness, "there has been a good deal of glib talk regarding the power of hypnosis to create dreams which, according to most researchers on this problem, are in all ways like spontaneous night dreams." Follows a brief reminder of the often-quoted hypnotic symbolization of the female genital through a traveling bag labeled as of homosexual interest, by the inscription "For ladies only," and the comment:

> This was certainly a provocative outcome but scarcely proof that the response to a hypnotic suggestion to "dream" is a psychological product comparable in all significant qualities to the condensed, delicately wrought content which issues from the dream work during sleep. It is curious that investigators appear to have taken it for granted that the hypnotic suggestion to "dream" actually issues in a dream. It is as if the belief in the magic power of hypnosis overwhelms the investigator as well as the subject and thus, when the subject responds with a production which often resembles a night dream, it is assumed without further question that there is no difference between the two.

Yet there is. A comparison between dream and hypnotic production is, as the author explains, a comparison between two groups of phenomena rather than between two phenomena; because neither the psychic experiences of the sleeper nor those of the hypnotized person are homogeneous in themselves. On the side of the dream Freud's indecision whether or not to believe in "fantasies during sleep"[3] as distinct from dreams is quoted with much justification; so is the author's recognition of the extreme variability of the influence of the censor upon the form of the product and her uncertainty regarding the necessary as well as the sufficient criteria for classifying a particular psychic production of the sleeper as a "dream." On the side of hypnosis there is its varying depth, "involving significant and varying changes in ego functioning," and there is, furthermore, the suggestion to dream, given by the hypnotiseur to the patient, which is "likely . . . . to produce further alterations." All in all:

> The response to the suggestion, "You will now have a dream," ranges from a slightly embellished reminiscence of an actual event to a production which at least on the surface resembles a classical night dream. By and large, these productions employ "primary processes" more than does normal, conscious, waking thought but less than does the "typical" night dream described by Freud. Thus, although a wide range of phenomena appears, it may be said, from the point of view of the formal qualities, that the average hypnotic dream takes a position which is intermediate between the conscious waking daydream and the night dream, with considerable overlapping at both ends of the range.

With respect to the psychic dynamics of either process Brenman reminds her reader of the fact, that "while the primary function of the night dream is to guard sleep, the motive power for the hypnotic dream derives from the will to comply, insofar as possible, with the expressed wishes of the hypnotist"—a much-needed reminder. And with regard to the relinquishment of motility by the ego, she emphasizes the equally fundamental difference "that

---

3 *Phantasien während des Schlafens;* literally: fantasies while being asleep. "Dream fantasies," the term used by Brenman, is a mistranslation.

whereas one of the prerequisite conditions for night-dreaming is the withdrawal of motor-cathexis, the maintenance or withdrawal of motor-cathexis for the hypnotized 'dreamer' is determined by the hypnotiseur." On the other hand there are "significant similarities" concerning "alterations in the defensive and in the synthetic functions of the ego"(?—This reviewer). The author's experimental studies, conducted jointly with Merton M. Gill and Robert P. Knight, showed these alterations in the hypnotized individual to be "highly variable in different subjects," to "fluctuate a great deal from moment to moment" which "perhaps they do in sleep as well" and to imply "by no means . . . . an obliteration of ego functioning." This is undoubtedly true; the relation between medium and hypnotiseur is regressive and in part of the nature of an identification; but it were none at all if the ego had been dissolved.

A survey of the techniques employed in inducing the hypnotized person to "dream" and a characterization of the results conclude the general and most valuable part of the paper.

Suggestions to "dream" are given in many different ways. The most frequent techniques described in the literature are: 1) the subject may be told simply, "Now you will have a dream"; 2) he may be posed a specific problem or topic about which to dream; 3) a posthypnotic suggestion may be given to have a night dream on a specific theme; 4) he may be asked to recall a repressed night dream; 5) he may be instructed to continue "dreaming" where a night dream has broken off. We believe that all of these techniques are, in a sense, what Ferenczi called "forced fantasies" brought about in an altered state of consciousness or, better, of ego functioning.

The second part contains a descriptive classification of hypnotic experiences ("embellished reminiscence"; "static

pictorial image"; "quasi-allegory"; and "quasi-dream")
and examples from clinical observation, which the reader
may find the more stimulating the more he is capable of
applying to them the full knowledge embodied in *The Interpretation of Dreams.*

V. THE "TELEPATHIC" DREAM

JULE EISENBUD *(Telepathy and Problems of Psychoanalysis,* Psa. Quart., XV, 1946); NANDOR FODOR *(Telepathy in Analysis,* Psa. Quart., XXI, 1947); GERALDINE PE-
DERSON-KRAG *(Telepathy and Repression,* Psa. Quart., XVI,
1947); and ALBERT ELLIS *(Telepathy and Psychoanalysis:
A Critique of Recent "Findings,"* Psa. Quart., XXI, 1947)
have contributed to this topic. The first three of these
papers, devoted not so much to the establishment of the
hypothesis of the occult but to its application, are hardly
within the competence of this reviewer, who has so far remained incapable of convincing himself of the existence of
the "paranormal." He has naturally, as has any analyst,
had his share of unexplainable experiences; but he has
never found them to be so *in principle* and therefore to require the assumption of "extrasensory" perception.[4]

As far as the last of the papers is concerned, it presents
a critique of the others and is rather instructive. Ellis attacks the three parapsychologists' reports on telepathic
dreams by examining them as to method and by assessing
their value as evidence; the three authors answer him and
he answers them in return. One can hardly follow the arguments back and forth without clarifying one's own
thoughts on the subject.

[4] Freud's own writings upon the subject appear as the least convincing
part of his work: he admonishes us toward keeping an open mind but he
does not present anything approximately conclusive.

One of the authors complains of a relative lack of interest among analysts, in the subject, and traces it to a "fear" of either a new psychic force or of "damage to their professional standing" through a public acknowledgment of their convictions. In doing so he would seem to establish still another hypothesis without sufficient foundation.

VI. THE "PROPHETIC" DREAM

HANS ZULLIGER (*Prophetic Dreams,* Int. J. Psa, XV, 1934) examines six dreams, commonly looked upon as "prophetic" and distinguished, in his opinion, from those considered by some as "telepathic" through the removal in time of the extrasensorily perceived object instead of in space. This distinction, a formal one, as it is, applies only to one of the dreams in the author's collection; in the case of the other five the perception is self-perception; the dreamer—to summarize a somewhat lengthy demonstration—hallucinates the direct or indirect representation of an intent, while he subsequently carries out in the form of a parapraxia, a symbolic or symptomatic action or a bit of conversion.

A feverish girl with a father fixation, afraid of abrogating her incestuous desires through a *marriage de convenance* which confronts her unconsciously with their consummation attends a meeting, against her better judgment, instead of staying in bed and recounts what she called a "strange" dream of the night before:

She was about to go for a country walk with her fiancé. Suddenly she saw a high wall and a heavy black gate opened. She went through in front of her future husband and heard the gate slam in his face with a violent draft. Thereupon she fell into an abyss.

Four days later, on the date of the projected wedding she dies of pneumonia. The unconscious suicidal intent hallucinated as unconscious wish fulfillment by the dreamer (and represented through allusion: wall and gate of the cemetery, falling into the grave; as well as through symbolization: entry into the mother and return to the womb) is in perfect accord with the successful suicidal behavior of the same individual when awake.

Another of Zulliger's cases epitomizes the genesis of the legend of the prophetic dream.

A woman close to the termination of her analysis and due to menstruate dreams of having a baby at her breast while delaying her period a week. In reporting the dream she experiences both a conviction of its prophetic nature and a *déjà raconté* and connects the two in such a fashion that the latter testifies to the former. She contends, self-deceptively, that she has told the analyst once before a similar dream, revealing to her the conception of a child (her son) and to "know" therefore, that the dream was prophetic. In other words: retrograde fantasying is put into the service of wishful thought.

Zulliger emphasizes that all the dreams represented wish fulfillments and obtained their "prophetic" character from the substitution of the future for the past.

JAN EHRENWALD (*Precognition in Dreams?* Psa. Review, XXXVIII, 1951) has a patient, "a man of 38 who works as a floor manager in a big department store," under treatment "for an anxiety hysteria." In a certain *situation* this man has a *dream,* which is subjected to an *interpretation* and followed by two *events.* We quote:

The Situation:[5] During the last nine months [the patient] had been subject to severe "attacks" of anxiety in

5 All italicization in these quotes is the reviewer's.

the subway and in the bus. More recently the attacks came over him also on crossing busy streets, in restaurants and even at the fountain counter of his store. Analysis showed that his symptoms were largely due to a defensive mechanism directed against unconscious homosexual impulses which were aggravated in the feared situations.

After initial difficulties the treatment made good *progress*. The patient had gradually become able to face repressed material without untoward emotional reactions and to overcome much of his anxiety although he had not been able as yet to go about his business without being accompanied by a friend.

His dreams showed unmistakable evidence of positive transference. At that time—in the fourth month of psychotherapy, consisting of three sessions a week—he produced the following dream.

The Dream: 11/5/47. I was in the store. There was a guy *who apparently worked for us*. I had the feeling he was after something, ready to hold up the place. He had a large flip-open knife, opening it, closing it, suggesting he is a dangerous fellow. I got scared, called for Mr. X. and Mr. Y. to catch the man. I myself retreated into the telephone box to call the police to get him. All of a sudden the whole situation seemed to have dissolved. The guy was sitting there, I was talking to him. It was a much more friendly conversation. He took out the knife, flipped it open. It was not large any more—just half an inch or maybe one inch long. I thought how foolish it was to be afraid of the knife. It was not nearly as dangerous as it looked. It was very small. . . .

The Interpretation: The patient's associations made the homosexual nature of the hold-up situation obvious. The phallic symbolism of the knife needs no further elaboration. The two men mentioned in the dream were his colleagues who used to accompany him in the subway or bus. His call for the police stood for his invoking the help of the therapist in overcoming his unconscious homosexual impulses. Again, the sudden change of the scene in which the large knife turned out to be quite

small and harmless was an obvious reference to the
therapeutic progress made, to his feeling that he was no
longer afraid of his repressed homosexual tendencies. I
felt the time had come to offer an interpretation to the
patient to this effect. This I did during the same session.
At the same time I encouraged him to try actively to
overcome his phobia. He left greatly relieved, whilst I
had the impression that an important step had been
made towards his recovery.

The Events: The next session was two days later, on the
morning of the 11/7/47. The patient was some five min-
utes late. He reported with an embarrassed smile that
when getting on the bus he saw a colored fellow sitting
next to him at the back of the car, take a knife out of his
pocket and open it quite unconcerned. It was a little
pen-knife, just like the one in the second half of the
dream. The patient added, "I feel quite uneasy, ready
to get panicky any time, keeping an eye on him. Then
he took an apple out of his pocket, cut it and started
calmly eating it."

The patient gave this account greatly amazed at the
apparent correspondence between parts of his dream and
the subsequent event in the bus. "The knife," he added,
"was like taken out of the dream. But please don't think
that I am suffering from hallucinations. Never has a similar thing happened to me before." He further added
that he had missed the previous bus by a few seconds.
That was the reason for his being late for our session.

Remarkable though the existing points of resemblance
between the two sets of events may appear, they are not
stringent enough to warrant any far-reaching conclusions. Yet on 11/17/47, that is twelve days after the
dream under review and a week after the sessions in
which the waking incident with the knife was discussed,
my patient recounted a second real incident involving a
knife. "Yesterday morning I was on the floor of the store
when some character walked in. He looked like a real
tramp, with a battered hat, disheveled shirt, with holes
in his shoes. He looked fierce, like a maniac, *I knew him
from before. He had come to our place about three or*

four times before. I always watched him whether he was not out for stealing. But as a rule he bought something: stationery, pencils or soap. This time he walked straight to the cutlery counter. I was just two counters away and saw that he picked up a large kitchen knife, 4-5 inches long and said something to the girl at the counter, though I could not hear what he was saying. At that he turned around towards me, looked at me and with a savage gesture brandished the knife towards his throat. I got very uncomfortable, in fact I ran downstairs to the basement. After a while I pulled myself together and went back to the girl at the cutlery counter. "What happened to your boy friend?" I asked jokingly. "Did he buy the knife?" The girl answered in the affirmative, adding still somewhat taken aback, "He said, 'When that guy bothers me I'll cut his throat open.' Then he paid and walked out with the paring knife."

The patient gave the account of this second incident hesitantly, with the same air of amazement as the first one, resorting to gestures to illustrate his narrative. A self-made man of average education, he had no philosophical bent and was certainly not in the habit of introspection. The analytical experience was his first encounter with psychological problems of any depth. His common sense told him that, apart from their significance brought out in the analytical sessions, dreams could not possibly have any additional "occult" significance. I may also add that he had no inkling of my interest in the matter; had never heard of psychical research, of Dunne's "Experiment with Time," or the like. Still, the repetition of the knife incident, linked up as it was with his dream, alarmed him.

I repeated to him the interpretation of the dream and suggested that both the first and the second waking incident involving a knife may have been due to his increased awareness of such objects in his environment and, therefore, largely to his own state of mind. This explanation, I said, should dispose of any superstitious misrepresentation of his experience and would also account for the apparent duplicity of the cases described.

The question is whether it really does so? . . .

Follow eighteen pages of speculation, searching and critical, upon precognition, the pros and cons of its existence, and of that of precognitive dreams. It would appear that among the author's many arguments there is one that he fails to pursue, although doing so might almost have spared him the others. His dreamer, he informs us, is improved; i.e., less phobic and more aware. "Both the first and the second waking incident involving a knife may," he explained to him, "have been due to his increased awareness of such objects in his environment and, therefore, largely to his own state of mind." If such a "waking incident" enters the sleeper's production it becomes "day residue" in a dream. *Unerledigte* (= unfinished; not, or not sufficiently, dealt-with or thought-out) thoughts of the day in particular are one category suitable to becoming a day residue—or, to accommodate our author, a "postcognitive" representation—in the dream. Is it not probable that the patient's original "scotomization" of men's handling pocketknives had in the course of his improvement been replaced by preconscious apperception? If it had, rather than being surprised, one would expect to find it elaborated upon as a day residue in the dream. Two of the author's data seem to support this explanation: (1) Deliberate exposure to apperception, undertaken upon command, proved intolerable to the patient even after the dream; it could hardly have been tolerable before. (2) In the dream the knife-flipping man "who apparently worked for us" is characterized through this clause as someone already known to the dreamer. The dream itself points, in other words, to a period of waking life preceding, not following it, as containing the material for the hallucinatory elaboration in the shape of the man with the knife.

There is more than that; none of it, naturally, conclusive. The omission of all of it by the author appears illustrative of a personal preference, encountered occasionally, for the "paranormal" over the normal.

LEO H. BARTEMEIER (*Illness Following Dreams,* Int. J. Psa., XXXI, 1950) contributes an interesting study of dreams preceding immediately an acute psychosomatic or psychotic condition. Pre-Freudian thought had linked the two as cause and effect until Freud showed that their cause was a common one and the dream the earliest manifestation of the condition. "It is incorrect," Bartemeier quotes Jones, "to regard the dream as the cause of the symptom that subsequently arises. They both have a common cause in some buried thoughts. The same thoughts can come to expression in both a dream and a neurotic symptom, thus illustrating the near relationship of the two."

Two of Bartemeier's *examples* may be quoted here as illustrative of his own conclusions:

(1) A married man who suffered from obsessional thoughts of mutilating and murdering his wife and daughter continued in analysis for many months with no improvement until after he had the following dream: He dreamed he was crying intensely. The dream awakened him and he was immediately suffering from one of his typical migraine headaches. He expressed the conviction that the dream had awakened him because of the intensity of his crying, and he said he could not remember ever having cried so hard; that "every bit of me seemed crying." This re-enactment of his infantile rage against his mother led to the working through of his repressed hostility to her and a rather rapid alleviation of his obsessional thoughts against his wife and his daughter. After several years he has had no recurrence of his migraine. The dream and the acute reaction represented a crisis in his analysis, and both were manifestations of a marked change in the transference relationship which had been under way for several days. Whereas he had regularly identified me with his father whom

he loved and admired and who had meant so much to him, a change in my own disposition towards him had ushered me in as his mother whom he hated so intensely.

(2) A young mother awakened in terror from a dream in which she was helpless to prevent the drowning of her second daughter. Upon awakening in the morning she felt strange and remained in a state of detachment for several days. "Everything seems unreal and I feel removed and at a distance." She had been hospitalized six years previously because of an acute schizophrenic psychosis during which she made several attempts at suicide by hanging. She had come to analysis because she felt she had never completely recovered from this illness. She always saw herself in the child who drowned in the dream. This child had been illegitimately conceived, and this fact was a source of much unhappiness to herself and her husband. She identified herself with the child through her life-long feelings of having been unwanted by her own mother. The acute reaction she experienced following the dream was the way she had felt during the onset of her previous psychosis. She was most fearful she would again become psychotic and the clinical picture was that of a pre-psychotic state. In her fourth year she had been rescued from drowning and again in her eleventh year she had almost met the same fate. She suffered repeated attacks of pneumonia. Both the dream and the acute reaction were the gross indications of an abrupt change in the transference relationship which had been in evidence much more subtly for several days previously. This was a repetition in miniature of her previous psychosis which had occurred after her narcissistic object-choice had left for military service. That both these events were revivals of early infantile feelings can hardly be doubted. Within a short time during which she was able to recover her positive feelings in the analytic situation her symptoms disappeared.

[Bartemeier *concludes*] that the dreams which are followed by acute reactions during psychoanalytic therapy presage momentous events in the transference relationship. This is another way of saying that they represent attempts to cope with the very core of the patient's neuroses. That these deepest problems were stirred up by the work of the therapy can scarcely be doubted. The dreams of the sort I have been describing provide a true clue to the acute reactions which accompany them. In so far as the remnants of the dream-day are always present it seems highly probable that they constitute the precipitating cause of the acute reactions. Consequently, the "day-remnants" in these dreams are of greater importance than ordinarily, and they must be established and understood in these dreams more thoroughly than is our usual custom in practice.

One must agree with the conclusions drawn from these observations; one wishes merely that they were drawn more tightly. Both dream and symptom are acutely reactive to a current event. The event is a change in the transference, brought about by the analytic work and repetitive of a former traumatic occurrence which, in turn, is repetitive of a still earlier one in the dreamer's childhood. The nocturnal representation in the dream of the diurnal event is the day residue, and the latter thus obtains its central significance for the interpretation.

This makes one miss a detailed report upon the change in the transference and a detailed analysis of the day residue representing this change in the dream. The interchangeability of symptom, transference, and dream in expressing the same repressed conflict is, of course, based upon their regressive nature. What one would like to compare is how this conflict reflects itself in dream and transference, respectively, so as to understand the dream as a commentary upon the symptom. We are particularly in need of such commentary when the symptom is as yet insufficiently understood, as is, for example, estrangement. To name but one problem: is Freud's historical interpretation of the "far away" in the dream as "distant past" (childhood) applicable to the "I feel removed and at a distance" of the estranged? If it were, it would supply the historical regression complementary to the unknown topographical one in estrangement, and dream analysis would have contributed toward the elucidation of a pathognomonic symptom.

VII. DREAMS OF GETTING WELL

THOMAS M. FRENCH (*Reality Testing in Dreams*, Psa. Quart., VI, 1937) discusses dreams that have sometimes been termed "dreams of getting well" (*Genesungsträume*) and ascribes to them the faculty of reality testing. He is apparently not aware that reality testing implies a function of judgment (*Urteilsfunktion*) which the dream can never perform. What appears as the dreamer's judgment is actually the individual's when he was still awake; it is "material," as Freud has expressed it, "of the dream thoughts" taken over as "ready-made" products into the dream.

Freud has warned of this misunderstanding and has done so explicitly when, in Chapter VI of *The Interpretation of Dreams* he treated "The Intellectual Achievements in the Dream." While the author's thesis is thus but another example of the confusion of manifest content with latent thought—more precisely: with the material in which this thought is expressed—the type of dream dealt with in his publication deserves comment.

Dreams of getting well are rare but clinically important; in the reviewer's experience they occur, if they do, at a time when the wish to get well has been subject to analytic examination. They are apt to complement the patient's decision to get well in terms of the transference: parental demands which the child was unable to meet, sublimations which it could not achieve, are represented as met in the dream and achieved for the analyst as the parent. In the latent thoughts the analyst's recuperative proposition has obtained favorable consideration; in the dream the infantile wish to please the beloved and loving parent is experienced as fulfilled. Dreams of getting well are, in other words, dreams; they behave as such, and their apparent "prophetic" nature is explainable, therefore, by the general substitution, as Freud has expressed it, of the "present tense" for the "optative" in the dream.

French's own example is a satisfactory illustration. A patient, recovering from a psychotic episode, requests leave to visit a nearby city unattended. He is granted the leave but denied going alone; hospital policy makes it necessary to have him accompanied by his wife. The successful visit is followed by two dreams. In the first he meets the analyst and is told that he shall have more freedom in the future. In the second, a tripartite dream, he takes off, in the first part, from where apparently he had left off: he is back in South Africa, has his own house again and an administrative position. He is entertaining the boss and his wife; but, while he formerly always felt that he was a poor host, he now feels that he is a good one. In the second part, which explains the change through a transparent allusion, his central problem is further represented as solved. In the third part, however, he takes a shower in front of other people, "defecates," then catches the stool in his hand and it becomes a piece of soap with which he washes himself.

The following is an excerpt from the *author's comment* upon the dream:

> . . . We are struck by the ease with which the soiling impulse is succeeded by reaction formation without other evidence of shame or guilt in the transition. Instead of feeling ashamed, the patient seems to be boasting: "See, I can turn a stool into soap." It is as though he were performing a feat of magic before an audience. How can

we account for the ease with which the patient replaces
his shame by such a boast?

We have already mentioned that the patient is one of
the few patients in the hospital who is being analyzed.
Recalling this, we now discover that his boast is based
upon a real fact. The stool that becomes soap is a most
significant symbol of the analysis. To tell his dirty
thoughts has been most painful for the patient's fastidi-
ous ego. This dream represents the patient's first acceptance of the tolerance of the analysis for his anal-erotic
impulses. In this situation, telling one's dirty thoughts
is no longer an offense against good taste, but a means of
purifying one's self—which is the patient's conception
of being cured of his neurosis.

Thus in this dream the patient has hit upon an element in his real situation that offers a possibility for a
better solution of his conflict. In his infantile situation,
defecating in his bath could bring only shame and
humiliation. In the analysis, telling his dirty thoughts
is a kind of soap with which he can wash himself. The
dream has taken account of the difference between the
shame attaching to his soiling impulses in childhood and
the encouragement given to these same impulses in the
analysis, and has turned to the analysis as a solution for
his conflict. In other words, the dream work has succeeded in a bit of reality testing of which the patient has
not yet been capable in his waking life.

Reviewer's comment. One is tempted to take advantage
of this opportunity to suggest that metaphorical "interpretations" are not interpretations. Where they apply,
they are—as Freud has explained of the allegorical ones—
thought material intermediary between manifest content
and latent thought and seized upon by the dream work in
order to facilitate the "translation." Such an "abstract"
interpretation should, however, in Freud's opinion, come
from the dreamer himself; "the *correct* interpretation of
the substituted material," he writes, "must be established
with the familiar technical means." Is it not rather doubt-

ful that the terminal part of the dream, reported here, has an "abstract" meaning at all? Is it not almost certain that the "correct" one, found with the help of the dreamer's associations would have led to a childhood memory of this compliance with the demands for cleanliness and, in so doing, would have supplied the infantile model for the adult recuperatory compliance with the demands for social behavior?

VIII. INSOMNIA AND HYPERSOMNIA

Since the dream occurs in the sleeper and is, in its very essence, a reaction to a disturbance of sleep, analytic investigations of sleep disturbance cannot possibly be excluded from this review.

CHARLES DAVISON *(Disturbances in the Sleep Mechanism,* Psa. Quart., XIV, 1945) surveys insomnia as well as hypersomnia from the dual standpoint of neurologist and psychoanalyst: his contribution contains interesting examples of organic sleep disturbances, overdetermined psychically and amenable to psychotherapy with often striking results. Of the author's case reports the following—more or less paradigmatic and rarely extractable from ordinary analytic experience—deserves extensive quotation:

The patient, a middle-aged woman, married at nineteen and the mother of two healthy sons, had been suffering for two years from attacks of compulsive sleep of varying depth and duration accompanied by intractable nocturnal insomnia.

Six months prior to her present illness, she experienced extreme drowsiness and weakness during the late afternoon hours, whereupon she had to go to bed and sleep for as long as fifteen hours although she had

had an adequate amount of sleep on previous nights. One day no one was able to arouse her. She awoke spontaneously forty-eight hours later with no memory of the episode.

Since then there have been numerous such occurrences. The patient while trying to fight her desire for sleep, simply falls to the ground and sleeps—either peacefully or most fitfully—uttering phrases or banging her head against the rails of the bed. Upon falling asleep at night she suffers from nightmares, seeing "monsters and people with horrible faces."

Neurological examination disclosed dragging of the right foot on walking; coarse, irregular tremor of outstretched hands, more marked on the right; right hemiparesis; right hypalgesia with sensory disturbances for all modalities of the right side of the body and face; right hyposmia; diminution of hearing in the right ear. There were no pathological reflexes.

Laboratory data including electroencephalographic studies were negative. There was no difference between the waking and the hypnotic electroencephalographic tracings.

While under observation the patient's behavior was normal except that on some days she seemed dull, whining, sulky, childish and on the verge of a tantrum. Such moods and personality changes were often either the forerunners of, or merged into, a drowsy state. On such occasions her movements were slowed; her face was pale and presented a drawn, haggard appearance; the eyelids drooped and the eyes were glassy. During this state she vomited persistently, complained of drowsiness and weakness, and occasionally fell, sustaining injuries which were nearly always localized to the right side of the body. She either recovered from these drowsy periods or lapsed into deeper somnolence. Neither in her normal state nor during somnolence did she reveal her thoughts. When interviewed she appeared tense and violently scratched and tore at her right arm, breast and external genitalia; she was not aware of these acts until they were brought to her attention. In subsequent interviews, when she was reluctant to speak of a scene dealing with intercourse, she lapsed into a semiconscious state in which she re-enacted some of it. Upon regaining consciousness she was unaware of what she had done.

Hypnosis was induced with ease whereupon she was able to recall some of the amnestic gaps. One day she related the following dream:

I was tied down on a couch with a rope and forced to have intercourse. I had to have it twice. I struggled and kicked. I don't know with whom.

Analysis of the dream revealed that she had had sexual relations with her father from the age of six until forty-two when she became ill. The first experience was forced upon her and produced terrific fear. At the age of nine or ten, she became less frightened by the sexual act and experienced intense jealousy of her mother, especially after she had witnessed several conjugal scenes between her parents. At twelve and one half she seduced a boy of sixteen; at nineteen, because of her father's objections to this boy, she married another man but continued to have extra-marital relationships with both her father and her first lover. She considered her husband an inferior person and when she had intercourse with him she thought of her father and her lover, both of whom were "violent and passionate" and practiced certain sadistic acts which she missed in her husband. Her present illness began with the death of her lover, twenty-eight years after her marriage; her somnolent state evidently represented her desire for sexual gratification with him. After relating the story of her incestuous relationship, her condition improved. The attacks of drowsiness ceased completely, the vomiting and falling episodes became less frequent, and her nocturnal sleep improved. In the past three years she had only three attacks of somnolence and a few drowsy spells.

The report, representing a particularly successful instance of "mixing the gold of analysis with the lesser metal" of psychotherapy and hypnosis, is interesting in many respects. It shows "acting out" in life as well as in the transference in a psychotic exaggeration; it exhibits organic subcortical lesion as confined, pathogenetically, more or less to furnishing the "somatic compliance"; and, in describing the obtainment of a particular therapeutic result, it presents an example of "neuropsychiatry" as it should be practiced.

OTTO FENICHEL, EMANUEL WINDHOLZ, CHRISTINE OLDEN, FRANCES DERI, ANNA MAENCHEN, BERNHARD BERLINER and ERNST SIMMEL *(Symposium on Neurotic Disturbances of Sleep,* Int. J. Psa., XXIII, 1942) have treated neurotic sleep disturbances—insomnia, hypersomnia and related conditions—in the form of a Symposium. For the purposes of a brief orientation about the proceedings it is perhaps best to borrow Fenichel's summary, in which he explains that Windholz undertakes an attempt "to bring order into the multiplicity of problems involved and to make some practical suggestions as to how they may be approached. . . ." Olden and Deri present clinical contributions; the former some case observations of common sleep disturbances and their analytic cure, the latter the "case history of an unusual sleep phobia." Maenchen, in addition to this, investigates pavor nocturnus; Fenichel "summarizes the problems and the approaches to their solution," and Simmel (it must be added) contributes to the discussion some original ideas concerning various pathological states of "sleep."

Since a more extensive characterization of all of these papers would necessarily transcend the available space, two of them may be singled out on the strength of the fact that they represent, when combined, a comprehensive, if cursory, treatment of almost all the conditions involved and all the present psychoanalytic approaches to their understanding. They shall be summarized hereinafter under two titles, with which the reviewer intends, at the same time, to honor the memory of two friends.

Otto Fenichel: On Insomnia (Abstract). Insomnia is quite generally based on the impossibility of complete relaxation, brought about by inner causes. Clinging to certain cathexes—despite the wish to sleep—may have the same effect as continued tension in specific muscles; that is, either the state of sleep is not attained or, if it is, the function of sleep is disturbed and the effect on the organism is enervating rather than refreshing. . . . The same effect that an uncomfortable position or unconscious motor impulse can produce is even more frequently achieved by unconscious stimuli which are no longer under the control of the conscious wish to sleep and which still retain their cathexes. Dreaming serves the purpose of making sleep function when the cathexes are too strong. They are not necessarily the cathexes of repressed wishes (acute worry of affect-laden expectation, agreeable or disagreeable, in particular sexual excitement without gratification, also causes sleeplessness), yet in neurotic insomnia the unconscious "sleep disturbers" *prevail*. Why then is the neurotic not invariably an insomniac? In the first place, he frequently is; in the second place he may have learned to "neutralize" the disturbers; finally "constitutional" factors may contribute. But this question still awaits, as does that of dream frequency, its answer.

The best-known form of insomnia is the *sleep phobia*. It is the fear of the mobilization of repressed instinctual impulses during sleep or while falling asleep, and frequently starts with an anxiety dream of traumatic effect and causes the ego to fear dreaming as though it were an instinctual temptation. Inasmuch as voluntary control of motility is lost during sleep, it is first and foremost the fear of forbidden instinctual *actions* which can assume the form of fear of sleep. Sleep phobia in bed-wetters or former bed-wetters is often a fear of repeating their enuretic performance or, in adults the fear of nocturnal emissions; i.e., of a form of masturbation of doubtful permissibility from the standpoint of the superego. Falling asleep, in particular, is apt to "re-vivify archaic levels of ego-consciousness," of "erotic temptations involving the mouth, skin and temperature" and representation of "excitation experienced in the earliest period of development of the infant." A specific instinctual temptation is the remembrance of a "primal scene," which "likewise took place at night when the child was supposed to be asleep."

In contrast to temptations, "some punishment or catastrophe, associatively connected with certain instincts, that are for that reason considered dangerous, is likewise represented in the state of sleep." And, deprived of locomotility, one is unable to flee from the danger. Loss of consciousness may, furthermore, in itself "bear the meaning of castration." Sleep and death, falling asleep, and dying are equated in the unconscious.

Sleep rituals are attempts at protecting oneself against all these dangers; their analysis reveals the paricular kind of danger to be warded off. In the case reported by Mrs. Olden in the symposium, the passivity inherent in falling asleep constituted the threat; the patient, when taking her sleeping tablets, had a feeling of being master over her sleeping or not sleeping, and of having excluded, by means of an active measure, her unconscious fear that she might lose her self-control and be passively overwhelmed.

Ernst Simmel: On Hypersomnia (Abstract). Sleep—a psychobiological function, a means of establishing and maintaining the instinctual equilibrium of the ego—is a restoration process from the "physical and the mental point of view. Since it affords the ego recovery from inju-

ries to its narcissism, past and present, by means of nightly
regressions to earlier stages of its development, and since
it does so under conditions of a temporary denial of reality
combined with a blocking of the outward motor brain-
centers, the ego is apt to employ this psycho-physiological
method of defense against an environment hostile to its instinctual demands under conditions other than going to
sleep at night." Syndromes, such as "hysterical and epileptic attacks, twilight states and narcolepsy of psychogenic
origin" share with nocturnal sleep in the "temporary
auto-erotic or narcissistic withdrawal on the part of the ego
through a refusal to perceive consciously stimuli from the
external object world." The study of sleep disturbances
contributes, therefore, to the study of all these conditions.

It is necessary, however, to distinguish "between the disturbance of the various stages of depth of sleep" (only a
certain depth corresponds to prenatal existence), since even
sleeping medicines are selective in this respect; they pro-
mote separately either falling asleep or deepening sleep—
effects equivalent, psychologically, to a "protection against
stimuli from without or within," respectively.[6] It is only
the deepest sleep that is probably dreamless and identical
psychologically with existence in the womb. The study of
the various stages of ego regression and depth of sleep will
contribute to an understanding of the psychoses. Schizophrenia, for instance, "may be viewed as a disturbance of
the waking condition on a grand scale," and "the psychotic
process might at least be associated with a disturbance of
the temporary ability to regress through sleep."

All seizures, accompanied by a transient loss of consciousness are "nothing but attacks of sleep."[7] The hysterical attack, in particular, seems related to the initial stage;
the loss of consciousness repeats that associated with or-

6 An oversimplification of doubtful value (Reviewer).
7 *"Nothing but . . ."* ? (Reviewer).

gastic climax brought about through masturbation. The disturbance in falling asleep is traceable in these individuals (who are also apt to experience, when falling asleep, sensations of being abruptly awakened combined with the feeling of losing consciousness) to "earlier interferences with the infantile masturbatory orgasm itself"—interferences "in *flagrante delicto* and accompanied with the threat of castration." To the phobic reaction of the insomniac of this type corresponds the exhibitionistic elaborations of the hysteric, who exposes "triumphantly, as it were, the masturbatory orgasm, uses it as a means of inducing a state of sleep and obtains, thus, a hallucinatory satisfaction of repressed infantile sexual wishes by internal perception."

The psychogenesis of hysterical twilight states and somnambulistic attacks is of a similar nature. The somnambulist elaborates upon environmental stimuli as upon symbolical expressions of repressed wish fantasies; it is the symbolical disguise of the outside world as a derivative of the inner psychic world that appears to induce the superego to diminish its preconscious censorship and to "permit outward motor-innervation for the purpose of infantile instinctual gratification." Yet the superego restricts this permission to the lower limbs, legs and feet, because they are "the means for flight, whereas the upper extremities, arms and hands, are the executive agents of aggression."[8] It is the "gaining access of derivatives of unconscious id-impulses to the pre-conscious from which outward motor-discharges are set in motion as well as the loss of consciousness" that liken somnambulistic and twilight states to an orgastic instinctual gratification.

In epileptic seizures the defense through sleep is directed

---

[8] How about somnambulistic *actions?* Eisler (whom Simmel quotes in his paper) reports on a girl who undresses, drinks, and uses the chamber in a somnambulistic condition (Reviewer).

predominantly against aggression. The analysand became tired, drowsy or even fell asleep in defense against aggressive impulses in the transference; and certain individuals, "especially if they share a bedroom with the object of their suppressed hostility cannot fall asleep (for fear of losing control over themselves) or wake up immediately when their aggressive dream hallucinations become too transparent to themselves."

"Sleep and the performance of overt aggressive acts seem to be mutually exclusive." But the sleep must be deep enough to exclude "pre-conscious perceptions" from without and, if possible, that of "additional urgent aggressive tendencies" from within. If it is not, "dream work" must succeed in "depriving the destructive ideas of their actively aggressive character." (Which is why we are apt to dream of the objects of our murderous wishes not that we kill them but that they have died and we mourn them.) Two disturbances of the waking state—epileptic seizures and narcoleptic attacks—follow this pattern. Of the two the former is, of course, more deeply regressive; it reproduces the stage at which the infant could discharge his rage only by unco-ordinated movements. A morphine addict whom Simmel observed, for instance, reacted to the first and abrupt withholding of the drug in this ontogenetically early fashion by producing an epileptic attack.

The addict's need for the drug is, in essence, likewise that for a repetition of the orgastic sensation of infantile masturbation. The repressed unconscious fantasies, attached to the latter are, however, decidedly of an aggressive and destructive nature. It was the sexual climax that had once served "the purpose of introverting[9] aggressive intention." Small wonder that these individuals become insomniacs when they are being weaned. It is now the sleeping

[9] One misses an explanation of this term as employed here (Reviewer).

drug that enables them to fall asleep while safeguarding them against committing aggressive actions. They have relinquished the "auto-erotic, narcissistic possibilities of consuming their destructive energies during the day." And it is thus that they frequently have no other choice than to revert to their original drug or to "turn to the most severe addiction I have ever seen—that of sleeping drugs during the daytime."

IX. "DREAM BEHAVIOR" IN THE CHILD

MARTIN GROTJAHN (*Dream Observations in a Two-Year-Four-Months-Old Baby*, Psa. Quart., VII, 1938) renders a vivid and highly instructive report on a child's self-expression through play as well as through speech and gestures, and while asleep, half asleep and awake. He terms all of it "dream observation" and justifiedly so, because what the child can be heard to say in his sleep or when somnolent, while being taken up by his mother, informs one certainly of his dreams. And when awake and at play, he still enjoys ever so often the dreamer's privilege of hallucinatory experience. His language—as that of the dream—has no grammar: 'Sheppy! Poor! Supper! Porch! Spoilt!" means "Sheppy, the poor dog, lost his food on the porch and spoiled it." He points out a bird on the ceiling ("See, see, look, look, peep, peep, there see?") which had actually been there yesterday, after straying into his room, but is no longer there today; he hallucinates it, in other words, as the dreamer may do with a "residue" from the day before.

Some of his dreams, on the other hand, repeat excitements and shocks from the day or elaborate upon dangerous situations. After he had seen two puppies having a bitter fight over his mother's gloves, and had gone with them for a ride, he said in his half-sleep of the same night, "Wow-wow, ran, gloves, ride, car!" But it was not only excitement and thrills that he repeated in his dreams. After he had learned to be careful not to cross the street, and always to watch out for cars he mumbled during sleep, "Watch out! Careful! Cars!"

"The conclusion," Grotjahn writes, "appears justified that in children, play, fantasies and dreams are very closely related to each other, and that what in an adult would be called hallucinations may be called vivid visual imaginations, very characteristic of infant thinking, and if such fantasied, hallucinatory form of memory is observed in a sleeping child it may be called a dream." A good part of these dreams, in particular those of food, are devoted to wish fulfillments; but others are not. They show the child, as the author demonstrates rather convincingly, "struggling with strong and strange emotions which it could not work through during the excitement and rapidity of reality and which consequently he had to repeat and work through more completely in his dreams."

MARTIN GROTJAHN (*Laughter in Dreams,* Psa. Quart., XIV, 1945) examines a subject to which, one must admit, even the smallest contribution is welcome. Freud's economic formula, equating the energy discharged in laughter with that saved through a temporary relinquishment of inhibition, is well known. Beyond that, nothing is; neither the nature of the affect nor the conditions for its development in the dream. The only example in *The Interpretation of Dreams*—an observation of Ferenczi's—is one of transformation of affect; the dreamer laughs when he should cry and sob; its analysis leaves one dissatisfied, it appears incomplete. Grotjahn supplements: "Freud did not emphasize the expression of hostility in the laughter of this dreamer who laughs in the face of death. The conversion of passive suffering into active aggressive laughter is successful dream work." Very true: but so is much transformation of affect.

Of the four examples of Grotjahn's own observation the following may be quoted in full:

> The next variation of the laughing dream is so obvious in its motivation that it may be illustrated by one short example. A married woman of twenty-six, mother of one child, in analysis because of marital difficulties which were the expression of a character neurosis, had the following dream: "I came to your office and you were very drunk and silly. You made fun of me and everything I said made you laugh harder. I got very angry. . . ."
>
> In this dream [Grotjahn comments], the emphasis is on the transference. Undisguised, the action takes place between dreamer and analyst. There is hardly any symbolism involved, drunkenness standing as an almost unsymbolic representation of what the patient thinks about her analyst. The patient at that period of her analysis feared she might get along too well with her analyst. The dream anticipates the day when she would talk about her "silly" feelings toward the analyst and probably be laughed at and humiliated. Realizing this she gets very mad and awakens. Such undisguised transference dreams usually occur in the first part of analysis before the patient develops enough confidence in himself and his analyst to discuss his positive feeling toward the analyst as frankly as other kinds of emotions.

They do indeed. But they are not generally distinguished by the occurrence of laughter. Their particular interest within the scope of the present monograph lies in the fact that they restrict the validity of Feldman's observation (cf. pp. 26 f.) that the analytic hour, when dreamed about, is necessarily "disturbed by others."

Grotjahn's chief tenets are: "Laughter does appear in dreams, and its psychodynamics are the same as in waking life. . . . The dream is essentially the fulfillment of varied wishes; . . . In certain stages of awakening it may be that certain parts of the ego are functioning while others are still 'sleeping.' During the moments of awakening, the ego is re-integrated. Laughter in dreams constitutes such partial awakening. Intrapsychic perception—an important ego-function—is partially restored, the ego recognizes the hidden meaning of the dream-disguise, and the condition under which laughter arises obtains. . . ."

MARTIN GROTJAHN (*The Inability to Remember Dreams and Jokes,* Psa. Quart., XX, 1951) remarks upon a similarity between dreams and jokes to which Freud has not called attention: both are often forgotten and therefore cannot, to the discomfort of the individual who would like to tell them, be told. "Listening to a joke," the author points out, "is a passive experience; to repeat it to another is an act of wit and may require stricter censorship."

Very true; but there is, as far as the dream is concerned, an additional difference between the passive experience and its active reproduction: he who dreams is asleep; he who recalls a dream is awake. One question, to be answered is therefore: is what Freud in the case of the dream has termed the more efficacious "binding" of instinctual energy after its temporary release, applicable to both dream and joke? Must both be repressed again because instinctual discharge—through hallucination or laughter, respectively—has restored an economy upon which the individual is, for the time being at least, dependent?

Part Two

APPLIED DREAM INTERPRETATION

In this section a few examples are briefly reviewed illustrating the application of dream interpretation to anthropology, psychotherapy, characterology and diagnostics.

Students of the first chapter of the unabridged edition of *The Interpretation of Dreams*—a chapter treating the "pre-Freudian" literature on the subject from antiquity on—will appreciate the supplement to it presented by GERTRUDE TOFFELMIER and KATHERINE LUOMALA (*Dreams and Dream Interpretation of the Diegueno Indians of Southern California*, Psa. Quart., V, 1936) in their description of theory and practice of dream interpretation of the Diegueno Indians of Southern California, where the "dream doctor" employs not only his patient's, but his own dreams as well, for the treatment of all manner of conditions.

SARASI LAL SARKAR (*A Study of the Psychology of Sexual Abstinence: from the Dreams of an Ascetic*, Int. J. Psa., LXXIV, 1943), reports and interprets four dreams from the diary of a disciple of a Hindu Saint. Written a hundred years ago, the diary records the struggle undergone by its author while training to be an ascetic. It contains passages such as these: "The character of a person is tested by his dreams. When you find in dreams that you can remain calm amongst temptations, you are proceeding to-

wards the right state. If you find even slight mental disturbance you will understand that your inward weakness
is not gone. *The irrelevant elements of many dreams have
significance.*[1] It is good luck to dream a good dream.
Through a dream a mental state can be attained within
a short time, for which lengthy mystic practices would
otherwise be necessary."

The four dreams, well chosen and on the whole com-
mented upon expertly by the author, read in part more
like stories than dreams (Freud's "fantasies during sleep"?),
which may be due to the fact that the dreamer spent much
of his waking hours in a regressive state produced by the
mystic practices of his religious training. They show the
Hindu a human, subject to the same "primal fantasies,"
the same "complexes," and expressing himself in the same
symbolic vocabulary as his fellowman in the West. And
they demonstrate that, although "ascetic" and analytic
procedure have different aims, both employ dreams for a
similar "diagnostic" purpose.

GÉZA RÓHEIM (*Dream Analysis and Field Work in Anthropology*, Psychoanalysis and the Social Sciences, I, Int.
Univ. Press, New York, 1947; and *Technique of Dream
Analysis and Field Work in Anthropology*, Psa. Quart.,
XVIII, 1949) furnishes colorful illustrations of the work
of the anthropologist as interpreter of the dream. In the
last of the two articles, in particular, he describes the
deviation from standard technique, forced upon the inter-
viewer by the method of his investigation as well as by the
nature of its subject. The intelligent English-speaking
Navaho, chosen as an example, who is "used to working
with anthropologists," tells his dream and informs one
in "associations" of the persons appearing in it and of
their background. The place of associating proper is taken

[1] Reviewer's italics.

by a "story" that the subject is asked to relate—"any story he chooses"—while being told "that we are finished with the dream." Day residues are most difficult to obtain. The subject does not understand questions about them and is apt to state that "the day was like all other days." The investigator has to supply the events (fights, rituals or the like) that took place and have entered the dream. All in all, Róheim concluded, dream interpretations performed "even by the analytically trained anthropologist can never be as detailed or deep, and as personal, as those obtained in clinical analysis."

STEPHEN SCHOENBERGER (*A Clinical Contribution to the Analysis of the Nightmare-Syndrome,* Psa. Review, XXXIII, 1946) follows Jones in a threefold combination of definitions, describing (1) "a heavy weight lies on the chest of the dreamer, who" (2) "feels unable to move" (3) "and breathe." Distinguishing "nightmare" from "anxiety dream"—*Alptraum* from *Angsttraum*—the author studies a case of it and arrives at a general interpretation: "The nightmare attack is a reoccurrence of the experience the dreamer had when he witnessed the primal scene. The nightmare, the mother with a phallos, represents the cohabitating parents. On account of his oral trauma, the patient perceived the primal scene in oral-sadistic interpretation. The nightmare inflicts a talio-punishment, in correspondence with this perception, upon the dreamer: the attack is directed against his *chest* and executed so as to kill him. The dreamer behaves as he did on the occasion of the primal scene: he evades excitement by stopping breathing and pretends to be dead, by being motionless. Thus we were able to interpret the three symptoms, resulting from the nightmare-syndrome."

A report on the study would, up to this point, belong under the heading of "typical dreams." But the author, taking his cue from the Hungarian name of the phenomenon, whose translation is "witches pressure" appends, again following Jones, "Anthropological References," and concludes with an "Outlook to Sociology" in an attempt to elucidate themes such "the horse in folklore," "the stony guest in the Don Juan legend," and the epidemic persecutions of witches.

MARK G. KANZER (*The Therapeutic Use of Dreams Induced by Hypnotic Suggestion,* Psa. Quart., XIV, 1945) reports on the interpretation of dreams, most of them induced in hypnosis in the course of the successful treatment occupying six weeks, of a soldier suffering from "hysterical dyskinesia." The patient, an erstwhile stutterer, had, after climbing a hill on a long training march, wandered off by himself, and, found later in a deeply somnolent state, had displayed, upon being awakened, almost continuous and rather violent movements of a choreiform type and a semi-purposeful nature (Jitterbug dancing, swimming strokes, shadow boxing). While his "belle indifférence" (G.I. version) foiled all therapeutic attempts, including the administration of sodium amytal, he proved amenable to hypnosis, and compliant to the extent that the first hypnotic command produced a posthypnotic improvement. This was, however, as far as the therapeutic influence appeared to extend until the hypnotist resorted to the suggesting of dreams.

The conribution made by Dr. Kanzer to the technique of a psychotherapy of this sort, lies in the principles that he evolved for the selection of topics to be dreamed about by the patient. The most general principle concerns the introduction of a "considerable measure of free scope for the patient." This is achieved, e.g., by first permitting the subject a "certain amount of free association" and in doing so to elicit the "dominant mood or idea of the moment" which is then allowed to enter the determination of the suggested topic. The latter can be specific or general—an alternative which again allows spontaneity to the dreamer. It is furthermore possible to exert influence upon the "amount of affect released in the dreams by selecting themes which excite or reassure according to the indications of the moment." And at times, of course, one can witness "the indirect reproduction of past memories, which are too deeply repressed to be obtained by direct questioning in the hypnotic state." Finally, Dr. Kanzer emphasizes a fact perhaps not always given sufficient weight in the study of dreams in hypnosis by stating explicitly that "the greatly varying dreams, which were produced in response to the same theme suggested by the hypnotist" and "the recurrence of certain trends in the dreams despite the different topics presented" testify to the "great influence" of the "unconscious drives of the patient" in "determining the hypnotic dream."

One wishes that with these valuable directions for the introduction of certain selected elements of psychoanalytic technique into the hypnotherapy of a "monosymptomatic" disturbance the author had concluded his contribution. Instead he advocates—this is hard to believe unless one has seen it in black and white—the preparation of "uncommunicative" analytic patients with hypnosis or "narcoanalysis," and the employment of either of these techniques (directly, or indirectly through a "collaborating psychiatrist") "during certain phases" of a psychoanalytic treatment. . . .

FRANZ ALEXANDER and GEORGE W. WILSON (*Quantitative Dream Studies: A Methodological Attempt at a Quantitative Evaluation of Psychoanalytic Material,* Psa. Quart., IV, 1945) employ "evaluation" of dreams as an instrument for the drawing of characterological profiles utilizable in the classification of certain "psychosomatic" conditions. The disorders investigated are almost exclusively gastro-intestinal; in particular, ulcers, constipation and diarrhea. In their search for economic criteria permitting them to assess the strength of opposing tendencies, maintaining the conflict and entering the determination of symptoms, the authors resort to recording the relative frequency of the occurrence of dreams expressive, in their opinion, of these tendencies in the patient. Their objective in doing so is the establishment of a relation between the prevalence of certain "tendencies" and that of certain psychosomatic conditions. The authors' conscientious (although ampli-fiable) criticism of their own method is not only a frank one, but is allowed by them to restrict the validity of their conclusions. The replacement of the concept of instinct or instinct derivative through that of *tendency*, and the reduction of libido and erotogeneity to one quality, that of the *vector*, with the help of which tendencies are divided into three groups ("intaking," "eliminating," and "retain-ing" tendencies) are explicitly stated. So are other theo-retical steps, through which subdivisions—of the intaking into a "passive receiving" and an "aggressive taking"; of the eliminating into a "giving urge" and a "sadistic type of elimination"; of the retaining into a "constructive" and a "destructive type of retention"—are obtained. If one is doubtful as to how much understanding a method based upon the abandonment of so much of psychoanalytic theory is able to yield, one finds oneself in the company of the authors, who admit of their tabulation that "it shows certain correlations without being able to account for the causal connections behind these quantitative correlations." And if one wonders how far an *evaluation* of dreams is capable of replacing their *interpretation*, one is assured that the method is employable "only in conjunction with the usual technique of psychoanalysis." The formulation, finally, of the results of the study is sufficiently general to be unobjectionable, and in accord with one's own impressions, gained from patients and acquaintances showing gastrointestinal symptoms.[2]

LEON J. SAUL (*Utilization of Early Current Dreams in Formulating Psychoanalytic Cases*, Psa. Quart., IX, 1940) attempts "brief psychological diagnostic descriptions, made independently of any correlation with symptoms," and concerning another "psychosomatic" condition: hypertension. The "first ten or fifteen dreams alone," he reports, "yield a satisfactory formulation, . . . from a sentence to a paragraph in length, of the main trends and their interrelationships. . . ." And they do so in spite of the fact that "very deep material or that which is only distantly alluded to in the manifest dream is not included." The author considers this method adequate for establishing "factors . . . of central importance in psychosomatic studies" such as "kinds and degrees of repression," the "status [?—The Reviewer] of the ego, . . . the conflict situation, the kind and degree of solution of the conflict, of repression and gratification, particularly as those appear in the manifest content of the dream." And he outlines his procedure quite distinctly within the framework of the analysis of one patient.

One is, of course, left to wonder what benefit the investigator of psychosomatic conditions derives from learning that the "analysis of four male cases of essential hypertension" bore out the preliminary evaluation of their first ten dreams by revealing "close similarity in the nuclear conflict and its status," as evidenced in "dreams of being chased by a man in a sexual situation with a woman, with no adequate means of escape or other solution repre-

---

[2] For a further expert discussion of "dream evaluation" see the review by Fenichel in *Int. Ztsch. f. Psa.*, XXII, 1936.

sented." The author reports the coincidence of these dreams with a peak in the blood pressure curve and that of "dreams, which ended in escape or regression," with the nadir; and asserts that he had "not found this conflict in just this form" in male cases without hypertension. The reviewer has not been able to identify this "nuclear conflict" as anything but—the oedipus conflict. . . .

SIDNEY TARACHOW (*The Analysis of a Dream Occurring During a Migraine Attack,* Psa. Review, XXXIII, 1946) is the proponent of a theory about "psychosomatic" phenomena in general and migraine in particular; the former "fall either into the syndrome of overmobilization or the syndrome of inhibition, depending on whether the neurotic interferences stimulate a hyperactive attitude or lead to an attitude of total defeat"; and the latter belongs to the second of the two classes of syndromes because it is "a disease of relaxation, inhibition or collapse of tension." The author contends that his analysis of a dream, dreamed during a patient's attack of migraine (which had started during the day but "lasted the rest of the night") shows this dream to be indicative of "a massive inhibition of various tensions" and suitable to be "correlated with the somatic fragment of inhibition of tension in the shape of cerebral vasodilation (migraine.)" The general background for such a specific conclusion—the ubiquitous inhibition of affect in dreams, termed by Freud "the second effect of the censor"—is not even mentioned.

VICTOR W. EISENSTEIN (*Dreams Following Intercourse,* Psa. Quart., XVIII, 1941) finds "dreams which follow coitus directly . . . useful in understanding and treating psychosexual disorders" because they "reveal the immediate factors responsible for lack of sexual satisfaction and for the resultant moods of instability and depression." He contends that the "considerable emotional significance . . . may be utilized in the interest of psychotherapy" and that during the resolution of neurotic conflicts "alterations in unconscious attitudes may be advantageously observed and clinical progress evaluated in the dream reactions to a standard heterosexual stimulus. . . ."

BEN KARPMAN *(Dream Analysis of a Constitutional Psychopath,* Psa. Review, XXXIII, 1946) reviews a long series of dreams of a psychopath—"Reaction dreams," "Heterosexual dreams," "Emission dreams," "Homosexual dreams," "Paraphiliac dreams," "dreams of Relatives," "dreams of Crime, Theft, Dishonesty, etc.," "dreams about Drugs," "Anxiety dreams," "Prison dreams," "dreams about Watches, etc.," "dreams of Guilt"—and concludes that his patient's "dream life . . . . has a characteristic structure of its own" and is "pathognomonically and diagnostically different from that of the normal, the neurotic and the psychotic." The above classification is quoted here in order to suggest that the author's method has little in common with Freud's, as, for instance, his comment upon an arousal dream—reminiscent in the beginning, although but faintly, of Dora's second dream, yet in the end distinctly of her first one—goes to show.

The dream (partly in excerpt):

The dreamer walks down a street with tall buildings on either side, one row of which has collapsed, fallen inward upon themselves in consequence of, perhaps, an earthquake. He is afraid, starts to run, as do the rest of the people, and comes to "some fireman who was rigging some sort of canvas with which he was going to save some people. He wanted me to step inside of the canvas which was circular in shape, and all covered with water. He said he would save me from burning. I was afraid to try it and started running away, then I awoke."

The author's comment (in full): "Here danger pursues him throughout the entire dream, first in the form of an earthquake and then in the person of a fireman whom he fears, although the latter claims that he wants to save him. This fireman with the canvas 'which was circular in shape and all covered with water,' and which he said 'would save me from burning,' has an ecclesiastical suggestion and may be reminiscent of by-gone attempts to reach him through religion."

This comment is paradigmatic for the replacement—encountered frequently at the present time in psychoanalytic communications—of dream interpretation, as Freud introduced it, by something else. If this "something else" is a method, it can only be characterized, negatively, as the relinquishment of practically all the essentials of the method established by Freud; and positively, with regard to one of them, as the substitution of the analyst's for the patient's associations.

Part Three

ADDENDA AND EMENDATIONS TO THE THEORY OF THE DREAM

The material included in this section comprises successful and unsuccessful addenda and emendations. An attempt to distinguish between them, to sort out true from
spurious additions and to indicate who corrects whom—
the author Freud; or Freud, if the author would only read
him, the author—is made in discussing the particular contributions.

Among the reasons for the scarcity of both true addenda
and true emendations there is one that the present reviewer cannot state nearly as well as he once saw it stated
in action. It was on the Belgian stage, and the hero, errand
boy for a bathhouse, had been charged with delivering a
bathtub, a towel and, since both were rented, a bill. When
the curtain rose, one saw him stop on his way making sure
that he had all three of these with him: *la baignoire, l'essuie-main, le calcul.* But the task proved too big; he could
not remain aware, simultaneously, of three disparate objects. Reassuring himself that he was carrying bill and
towel, he missed the bathtub until he discovered it, finally,
where it had been all along, on his back. And by that
time the towel was lacking. He went on, laying hold of
two, groping frantically for the third; his despairing voice
still refuses to leave the ear. *Où est le calcul? . . . Où est la
baignoire? . . . Où est l'essuie-main? . . .*

I should apologize for appearing facetious where I am

serious, and make haste to explain my irreverent reminiscence with the perplexing experience of the reviewer of these communications. *Almost all of the errors and misconceptions that in the end foil the authors' intent to emend and add to the theory of dream and sleep have been anticipated and answered by Freud himself in* The Interpretation of Dreams *or the writings supplementary to it.* Since the authors have read these works, it can only be that they have not studied them to the extent of integrating the necessary number of data. Upon second thought one remembers, of course, that in a discipline unsupported as yet by an adequate academic tradition, the labor of assembling these data into the spacious and intricate frame of reference of which they are part rests upon individual shoulders; that Freud's work on the dream alone is rather extensive; that his treatment of different subordinate subjects is uneven; that a general index, let alone a concordance, is lacking; and that there is not as yet even a correct English translation of *The Interpretation of Dreams.* Small wonder then, that the cryptomnestic contributions outweigh the original ones, and that much is discussed in print that belongs in classrooms.

I. CAN A DREAM BE KNOWN?

JULES H. MASSERMAN *(Language, Behavior and Dynamic Psychiatry,* Int. J. Psa., XXV, 1944) requests that one let *him* "venture upon the *dialectic* proposition that no dream as such has ever been analysed—or ever will be analysed— until we develop a technique of reproducing the dream sequence itself on a television screen while the patient is asleep. All we can do at present is to note carefully the patient's verbal and other behaviour patterns while he is talking 'about' his hypothetical 'dream' during some later

analytic hour, remembering all the while that his hypnagogic imagery has inevitably been repressed and distorted in recollection, that it is described in words and
symbols coloured by his experiences not only before but
since the 'dream', and that in the very process of verbalization his 'descriptions' and 'associations' are further dependent on his unconscious motivations in telling the
dream at all, his transference situation, his current 'ego
defences', his physiologic status and the many other complex and interpenetrating factors of the fleeting moment.
There is, then, no 'language of the dream,' . . ."

No, there is no such language; one would like to know
whether anyone ever said there was (except Stekel, whose
confusing book is not included in the list of references to
Masserman's communication). There is merely a script of
sorts; a "primitive medium of expression analogous to pic-
tography," as Freud called it, into which the dream
thoughts are translated by the dream work. Its comparison
with some media comparable to it, such as hieroglyphics
and Chinese picture writing, is to be found in Chapter XV
of the *Introductory Lectures*.

The "proposition" quoted above is not, however, either
Masserman's or dialectic. It is Freud's, has been set forth
by him in Chapter VII of *The Interpretation of Dreams*
and is expository to an inductive conclusion drawn from
an examination of facts. The result: if the dream *report* is
not "The Dream," the dream as *dreamed* is not either.
For they are both distorted under the influence of the same
institution (censor) and in the same fashion (dream work,
secondary elaboration). When there is less remembered
than dreamed—something of which one is often directly
aware—this assists the interpreter rather than hindering
him. It does so by *eliminating* uninterpretable as well as
impertinent content (elements dreamed either under too
high a "pressure of resistance" or owing their existence to

"secondary elaboration"); and by *introducing* new utterances of a resistance (doubt, "corrections," etc.) operated selectively against certain elements which are thereby marked as more directly derivatives of a latent thought than, e.g., their indistinctiveness would otherwise have suggested. No, the dream as such is not knowable; and we would not gain if it were. It is, after all, latent thought and not manifest content that we attempt to retrieve and to restore to the patient who owns it, whether fully awake or but partially so as a dreamer.

II. THE "NEGATIVE" IN THE DREAM

NANDOR FODOR (*The Negative in Dreams,* Psa. Quart., XIV, 1945) bases a communication upon what appears to be a twofold misunderstanding. He confounds manifest content with latent thought and the dream defined as hallucinatory experience with the thought fragments punctuating it and exhibiting all the characteristics of wakeful thinking. The same pen that wrote in the *Introductory Lectures:* "an unambiguous representation of the 'NO' cannot be found in the dream" had recorded almost two decades earlier as introductory to the clinical chapters of *The Interpretation of Dreams,* the "Dream of Irma's Injection" which contains no less than six negations. (The reviewer counted them for the purpose.) This dream, the very first one ever analyzed, testifies to what Freud has termed "the existence in any extended dream . . . of elements which have failed to partake in the transformation into sensory products [*ins Sinnliche*] and are simply thought or known by the dreamer as we are accustomed to doing when awake." It presents us in fact with a collection of different examples, sufficiently representative to deprive Fodor of all priority in regard to his own illustrations.

Freud *reproaches* Irma at the beginning for *"not* yet accepting the 'solution,' and 'friend Otto' " silently at the end, because "one does *not* give such injections that readily"; furthermore he *judges* that "she does *not* have to" (resist the inspection of her throat). "M.," however, says: *"No* doubt, it is an infection, but it makes *no* difference" [*es macht nichts*]; and Freud eventually conjectures "the syringe was probable *not* clean either." Negation, in other words, enters the manifest content of the dream at places where the dreamer does not hallucinate but thinks, either silently or aloud. Such thought may be ascribed to someone else, be distorted, elaborated upon secondarily, or be expressive of symbolization; what matters is that it has remained thought instead of becoming hallucinatory event.

Fodor, who has not clarified this for himself, discovers a "latent negation," which is, however, no more than an elliptic allusion (someone "said that the roof was beautiful and so clean," indicating that the *inside* of the house is "very dirty"), while his "concealed negative" ("so well-concealed that it only emerges from the patient's associations") is an example of the failure, mentioned above, to distinguish manifest content and latent thought. It is obvious, but apparently nonetheless necessary to point out here, that the negating thought may contain a "negation" in the particular sense established by Freud and treated by him in a separate study on the subject. It may of course do so, regardless of whether the thought had been dreamed or is contained in a later comment which the interpreter considers part of the dream. An example of Fodor: "An old woman dies and her daughter goes to see her. . . . She cannot be my mother; this woman in the dream is much older."

Since the dream *report* is thought before or while it is rendered, it can, naturally, employ negation in the description of a hallucinatory experience. Fodor:

. . . . I wanted to change my uniform in the bus. It was embarrassing but I tried, without success. *The blouse would not slip* over my shoulder so I put my uniform over my clothes. The bus went the wrong way. . . .

If one asks oneself why this particular wording is chosen in the report one may employ Freud's study as a key to the answer and suspect that the inhibition hallucinated in the dream is replaced in wakefulness by a "negation" in the sense of Freud's study because the blouse, a female garment, is unacceptable to the male patient whether asleep or awake. Inhibition, one form of indirect expression of a "no" in a latent dream thought is thus transformed into its equivalent, a "negation" in the direct expression of the same thought by the erstwhile dreamer. (The interpreter does not fail to confirm this equivalence indirectly through a parapraxia: he refers to the blouse in the dream as not slipping over *"her* shoulders". . . .)

The author feels that "it behooves us not to lay down rigid laws regarding mental manifestations." His material, however, validates Freud's discovery that the lack of a negative is among the characteristics of the primary process and, therefore, of the hallucinatory elements of the dream.

III. THE "TRAUMATIC" GENESIS OF THE DREAM

ANGEL GARMA (*The Traumatic Situation in the Genesis of Dreams,* Int. J. Psa., XXVIII, 1946) generalizes on an old finding of Freud, and by so doing is persuaded that he has made an original contribution. The "new point of view in the study of dream psychology" advocated by him is the opinion that "the traumatic situation does not only contribute to the dreams of traumatic neurosis, and those reproducing certain infantile traumatic situations" but "to all dreams" and that it is "the most important factor of all."

It is difficult to discuss this type of "emendation" without appearing pedantic. To begin with, the exceptions from the wish-fulfilling function of the dream conceded by Freud are not confined to dreams "reproducing certain infantile traumatic situations" and dreams of traumatic neurosis. They concern, as the unusually exact English translation of *Beyond the Pleasure Principle* by C. J. M. Hubback and Ernest Jones formulates it: (a) "dreams occurring during psychoanalysis that *bring back the recollection* of psychic traumata of childhood. This does not mean that they *reproduce,* as they may but need not, the traumatic *situation.*" (b) "dreams . . . . apart from analysis . . . . which in the interests of the psychical binding of traumatic impressions *follow the repetition-compulsion.*" This is still, at least potentially, further removed from the dream symptomatic of traumatic neurosis. Is it not significant that Freud, having gone so far, did not, himself go further? And should not anyone, who feels entitled to do so, furnish us with a detailed criticism of Freud's own arguments, set forth twelve years later, for abiding by the wish-fulfillment theory of the dream in spite of the repetition compulsion? The account is rendered in the first of the *New Introductory Lectures;* it contains both of Garma's cryptomnestic observations, that of the unpleasant character of so many dreams, and that of the attempt of the dreamer to attenuate this unpleasure by means of a wish fulfillment.

Why do people, Garma asks in effect, fail so frequently to allow themselves a good time in their dreams? "The instinctual gratification in dreams," he writes "is lacking in intensity. Dreams tend to be rather cowardly when it comes to getting satisfaction." "I kiss Aurea," dreams a patient. In reality he had not even dared to kiss Aurea although

Aurea had wanted more than that. (Oedipus complex. Aurea is representative, in the unconscious, of his mother.) "But why," and we quote Garma verbatim, "is he not bold enough to create a dream to destroy his inhibitions, making Aurea completely different from his mother, and in this way to have a happy and complete love affair with her?"

It is not the naïveness of the question that embarrasses a reviewer, but the consistent disregard of *The Interpretation of Dreams* in the author's search for an answer. Dreams, Freud has taught us, are most directly perceptive of the unconscious. If it is there that Aurea is the mother, she is it in the dream; and since the dream is a wish fulfillment, it allows the dreamer to hallucinate doing what he had been unable to do when awake: he dreams of kissing his mother in the shape of a woman as young and desirable as she had been in his childhood—the time into which the dream, executor of an unconscious infantile dream-wish, takes him back. There is, however, no dreaming without compliance to a "censor." And of the two censorial functions, one has been termed by Freud the "suppression of affect." It is thus that he has explained why not only "instinctual gratification" but *all* emotion is "lacking in intensity" in most dreams. Traumatic origin, as is demonstrated by the "traumatic dream," effects the opposite; the traumatic dream, a variety of the nightmare, is replete with affect and is terminated by arousal because of an "anatomical" damage to the psychic organization upon whose intactness ordinary dreaming depends.

J. O. WISDOM (*A Hypothesis to Explain Trauma Re-Enactment Dreams,* Int. J. Psa., XXX, 1949) formulates what he terms a "fundamental hypothesis" to the extent that "dreams are need-fulfilments or attempted pleasure-need-fulfilments" as follows: "A dream or Perceptualization during sleep is either an undistorted Perceptualization of the fulfilment of pleasure-needs alone, or a Perceptualization of them distorted by Condensation, Displacement, and Symbolization and modified by Secondary Elaboration, in both cases to preserve sleep against disturbance by a physical stimulus whether external or in the body, OR a Perceptualization of both pleasure- and punishment-needs, distorted by the same distortion mechanisms, to reduce pressure from the punishment-needs by distortion of all needs and by initial Perceptualization of the pleasure-needs alone, with the aim of preserving sleep against disturbance by punishment-needs aroused by the unperceptualized pleasure-needs." The reviewer has failed repeatedly in the attempt to clarify the above formulation by studying the communication, and must therefore leave this task to the reader. The article does not contain the analysis of a single dream, introduces several terms, and is confined exclusively to speculation.

Of the misunderstandings in it there is one demonstrative of the lack of adequate English translation of Freud and therefore of general interest. Freud is quoted as saying (in the first of his *New Introductory Lectures)* that in cases such as the unconscious fixation on a trauma the dream work *"fails to operate,"* which the author questions "if only on the grounds that where there is no dream-work there is no distortion, and therefore the interpretation should be obvious—which it is not." This is an argument against W. J. H. Sprott, the translator, not Freud. The original states in these instances that the dream work *"fails in operating"* (*"versagt die Leistung seiner Traumarbeit"*); in other words, that the dream work *fails in fulfilling its function.* One is almost the opposite of the other: Freud implies presence, Sprott absence of dream work, and Wisdom refuses, rightly, to be misled.

By way of a footnote to the formulations, quoted above,

one should perhaps append the author's definition of terms:

Perceptualization: ". . . . a mechanism by which it is primarily pleasure-needs that are expressed in imagery, ... primarily a process of forming pleasure-hallucinations."

Pleasure-need: "It will be convenient to write 'need' instead of 'wish.' The need involved is recognizably a need, in the way in which one may recognize a need in another person or in oneself. This does not necessarily preclude the use of 'phantasies of which a person, awake or asleep, is unconscious' as equivalent to 'need,' though some would prefer to distinguish these and say that only when a need is directly felt as such can it manifest itself as a wish. The reason why the change of terminology is convenient here is that the general result becomes easier to express: for it is natural to use 'wish' as an abbreviation for 'pleasure-wish,' so that a wish is either a pleasure-need or the acceptance of a pleasure-need. . . ."

Punishment-need (implicit definition): ". . . . the phrase is used for all factors that interfere with complete pleasure-need-fulfilment."

IV. THE DAY RESIDUE AND ITS POTENTIAL

EDMUND BERGLER *(A Third Function of the "Day-Residue" in Dreams,* Psa. Quart., XII, 1943) contends that the "day-residue"—besides supplying, as Freud has shown, the unconscious infantile dream-wish with representations, direct and indirect, acceptable to the censor—fulfills two more "functions." (The second of these had previously been proposed in "Instinct Dualism in Dreams," by Drs.

Jekels and Bergler, *ibid.*, IX, 1940.)[1] The two new functions are the representation, by the day residue, of a reproach from the superego and of its refutation. Or, to quote the author verbatim: "The day-residue present in dreams contains three elements condensed into one, varying only in a quantitative sense." In other words, three functions are served by the day residue: 1—"Package-wrapping for contraband articles," that is, id wishes (Freud). 2—"Symbolic representation of superego reproach" (Jekels-Bergler). 3—"An attempt to refute the reproaches of conscience" (Bergler). . . . The author found this "confirmed" in the analysis of "several thousand dreams."

The addendum is spurious. This time, *literally,* three essential metapsychological data have not simultaneously been kept in mind. Freud—with whom neither Bergler nor Jekels seem to entertain disagreement—ascribed the hallucinatory effect to the last of three phases in the manufacture of dreams. This phase takes place in the sleeper, is dependent upon the regressive nature of his psychic organization, and processes day residues as well as other material. The phase preceding it is the formation of the dream-wish. This may or may not occur during sleep; it consists in the employment of the preconscious day residues for the expression of an unconscious tendency *(Regung)* which becomes thereby preconscious. The first phase concerns mainly the day residue and consists in its "reinforcement" through the repressed unconscious to such an extent that it acquires the former's resistability to the wish to sleep. This initial phase, in which an impression of thought of the day before, through a "transfer" upon it of cathectic energy, becomes a potential day residue, may, but need not necessarily, occur while the subsequent

[1] This article does not require a separate review; the first part of its double thesis, concerning day residues, is reviewed in the text above; the second, epitomized in the title, on the occasion of Jekels' study on sleep.

dreamer is still awake. The ideational content, however, overcathected during this phase, is a product of the psychic activity of an individual in possession of a fully differentiated psychic organization. It is thus that the day residues —as Freud expresses it so frequently "the real [*eigentlichen*] disturbers of sleep"—own, as he termed it, "the whole manifoldness of our psychic acts" of which self-reproaches, apologies for oneself, and the comparison of oneself with what one ought to be are but a part. It is true that Freud, unacquainted with his as yet unwritten *The Interpretation of Dreams,* saw this before he saw anything else; and that it dominates, as is pointed out by Bergler, his comment on the "Dream of Irma's Injection." But it is also true that he distinguished it subsequently as "dream material," from the dream proper, product of the "dream work." With regard to *judgments* in particular— and what else is a "superego reproach" and its "refutation" —he has warned the interpreter explicitly of deception; they are dream material and belong to the latent thought not the manifest content, into which they were merely inserted as previously "completed formations."

Bergler, in other words, shows what Freud has discovered: that the day residue is a residue from the day; a remainder, that is, from a time where one had been awake, in possession of an ego, superego and id, and thinking thoughts, inconceivable without the participation of all three of these institutions. It is such thoughts that a day residue is, of course, likely to represent.

Bergler's *own* thesis would thus reduce itself to the postulate that a thought capable of appearing as day residue in a dream is representative of a conflict; in particular one between ego and superego. Such a postulate contradicts the observable facts. If the author thought not, he should at least have objected both to Freud's original enumeration of potential day residues, containing, e.g., thoughts simply not completed during the day owing to some "accidental cause" and "indifferent impressions of the day which have consequently been left unsettled," as well as to his later characterization of them as, e.g., "unsettled [*unerledigte*] wishes or fears, . . . intentions, reflections . . . . attempts to adapt to current tasks, etc." But he does not object; he merely quotes and remains unaware of the incompatibility of his contention with the variety of different thought processes representable by a day residue in the dream.

V. THE EGO IN FALLING ASLEEP

OTTO ISAKOWER *(On the Pathopsychology of Falling Asleep,* Int. J. Psa., XIX, 1938) has applied Freud's method of conceiving of a normal process by observing its pathological distortions with a degree of success rarely approximated since Abraham's day. His report defies abstracting, it must be read; a review can only bring it to the prospective reader's attention. The latter in order to place the particular form of disturbance of falling asleep investigated here might revert to the abstracts of Simmel's and Fenichel's papers, published five years after Isakower's, on "Hypersomnia and Insomnia" (see pp. 49-58). There Simmel speaks of disturbances "traceable . . . . to earlier interferences with the masturbatory orgasm itself . . . . *in flagrante delicto* and accompanied with the threat of castration . . . ," and Fenichel terms "sleep phobia" a "fear . . . . of masturbation of doubtful permissibility from the standpoint of the superego." Isakower has observed a certain, although infrequent, way of resolving this conflict by means of excessive regression: the "disturbing genital instinctual desire for the incestuous object" is replaced by the "harmless, not prohibited situation at the maternal breast or of intrauterine existence." Such is possible because at a certain stage of the process of falling asleep the condition of the regressively altered and temporarily overcathected body-ego becomes representative (although not exclusively) of this earliest gratificatory situation; and because, while at that time external perception is already practically relinquished, internal perception is still preserved. It is by virtue of these coincidences that the condition is experienced and enjoyed.

The record of it has the value of a Rosetta stone: it is articulate about the inarticulate nursling and informs us intelligibly of his chaotic world. It confirms what Freud has divined and described of it in the second of his *Three Contributions to the Theory of Sex:* dominance of the mouth zone; fusion of it with the skin, which contributes, as it were, tactile and kinesthetic experiences to those of the mouth; perceptions localized, simultaneously, as sensations in a particular zone of the body and as occurrences in a coterminous border zone of the outside world. From there "something big" and "round" is approaching, filling the oral cavity, although quasi-autochthonous to it, and impressible at the same time, by the hand. It is the breast; the original "object," indistinguishable, virtually, from whatever there is of an "ego." Thus, while of "doughy" consistency, it becomes "sandy" and "crumpled" when the mouth of the nursling is dry.

These are but salient features; the total picture, derived from all sensory spheres, is replete with fascinating detail, partly interpreted by the author and partly awaiting interpretation. Recumbent position is constant, hypnagogic (sometimes hypnopompic) or fever states are variable as prerequisites for its appearance.

There is one, among several, characteristics that distinguishes the phenomenon from the ordinary hypnagogic experience and suggests a proximity to the *aura* and to the *déjà vu:* the subject is curiously observant of his condition, which does not cease when attention is focused upon it, but impresses some as though it could be provoked and others as though it could be extended at will.

It is this particular trait, although supported by others, that guides the author toward his basic conclusions: the process of falling asleep, besides reviving archaic experiences which remain in most instances unobserved, causes not only cathectic increase but a cathectic alteration of the ego. The alteration consists, in the main, in (1) "a falling apart of the different parts of the ego and of its functions, and (2) in its re-differentiation." The latter "appears to begin somewhat later than does the dissociation of parts and functions. . . ." The withdrawal of cathexis from the environment into the ego is, in other words, accompanied by a cathectic redistribution inside the ego; in particular one "between the body-ego and the perceiving and testing of parts of the ego." The "observing institution becomes thereby more sharply opposed to the body-ego with which ordinarily it appears more closely connected." It is thus, that a body-ego, its boundaries blurred and fused with the environment, becomes an object of observation to a perceptive surface.

So much for economy and topography of the process. With respect to its dynamics, the author assumes that the intermittent cathectic surges *(Besetzungsstösse),* postulated for all perception by Freud, continue, although diminished in force and frequency, while one is falling asleep; and that they do so with the result of a "cathectic oscillation of variable quantities between the regressively altered body-ego on the one hand and the perceptive apparatus progressively voided of cathexis yet still preserved structurally, on the other." The hypothesis is completed by the assumption of a complementary "accretion of id-libido" to the ego—an assumption in good accord with the latter's archaic appearance.

In a period to come, when psychiatrists are determined to use analysis for the purpose of penetrating their subject, some investigators will revert to the author's remarks upon psychiatric matters, punctuating his paper. One impressive example concerns the juxtaposition of a report on the hypnopompic occurrence of the "phenomenon" by one patient and the association of a screen memory to it by another. The comparative study of the two documents produces the comment that in them "the sensory material for an experience of 'eclipse of the world' [*Weltuntergangserlebnis*] is already present but [that] it is not as yet *elaborated upon* to the extent of a *delusion*."[2] The decomposition achieved here, of the pathogenesis of a psychotic production as important as this into two separately observable phases, may, in this reviewer's opinion, at a future time prove the beginning of its further elucidation.

I have avoided quoting from Isakower's clinical records. They must be studied in full and compared in detail to each other if they are to become the composite observation upon which the author has drawn and from which he has derived his conclusions.

VI. THE EGO IN DREAMING

PAUL FEDERN (*Ego-Feeling in Dreams,* Psa. Quart., I, 1932) contributes an article, culminating in the following thesis:

In waking life, all power is returned to the ego, in particular the will. *The will is the turning of the whole active ego cathexis to particular activities, whether they be mere thinking or action.* To believe that the will is

2 Reviewer's italics.

only a foreknowledge of an event which would occur in any case is a completely erroneous intellectualistic conception, as Klages long since proved. The ego *as a whole* has at its disposal a certain active libido cathexis which it can send out or withdraw, and *this* is the will. Active bodily ego feeling in waking life represents the materially smaller permanent cathexis of the ego. In dreams it represents the will.

This thesis, representative as it is of the author's work, gave pause to the present reviewer, who found himself hesitating in making comment. One asks: what is an *active ego cathexis?* Is there a passive one, as there ought to be, and what is it? What is "will"? How, if the total ego cathexis were allotted toward an action, could there still be an ego to act? What is an active ego *feeling?* And, whatever it is, how can it, an experience, be equated with a "cathexis," a hypothetical process, of the "ego," a hypothetical institution? An experience is subjective; a dynamic process, a topographical entity are objective; they cannot possibly be the same.

Writing such as this does not, in other words, withstand reading; but it is one thing to say so to oneself and another to say so in public. One may, of course, argue that if an author commits his thinking to print his critic may do so; one may even consider him under the obligation. Yet in the present instance author and critic are of a different generation: one, pioneer and enthusiast, the other, trained and aware of the delusional tendency of theoretical thinking. It is impossible to review Federn's writings and do right by Federn; one has merely the choice between being unfair to a meritorious teacher of the past or to the serious student of the future.

Among Federn's merits is the selection of his subjects; he was sometimes the first to recognize the importance of a particular problem. In the present piece he attempts, if I understand him, to learn something about the ego from the study of the dream. The *first* section deals with the ego feeling as such. "Whenever an impression impinges, be it somatic or psychic, it strikes a boundary of the ego normally invested with ego feeling. *If no ego feeling sets in at this boundary, we sense the impression in question as alien.*" Note the unholy influence of the word. The German *Ichgefühl*, ego feeling, a pre-Freudian term, is no longer employable in analysis because "ego" has been differently defined. One must employ the synonymous *Selbstgefühl* and translate "feeling of self" lest a descriptive and a theoretical term are confused. Federn's "ego boundary" is an engaging expression but it denotes so little that it were better to wait until it could be defined in excess of Freud's "surface" or "system" (such as, e.g., Pcpt-Cs). The *second* section, comparing *Entfremdung* and dream state suggests another reminder concerning terminology: *Entfremdung* (estrangement) is a generic term; it includes depersonalization and derealization—or if it does not, it should, in the present reviewer's opinion. Freud does not use it so;[3] to him it is merely the German for derealization. Federn confuses the two, without, apparently, being convincing to Freud who four years later still calls the *Entfremdungen* "very strange phenomena, as yet little understood," and in comparing them to the dream confines the comparison to the "abnormal structure" and the "regular occurrence" of these "models of psychic disturbance" in the "normal."

From the *third* section, in which *Entfremdung* is compared to falling asleep and awakening, the following statements may be profitably contrasted to those of Jekels (see pp. 103-109).

> In dreamless sleep ego feeling is extinguished. . . .
> When an individual falls asleep rapidly, ego feeling is suddenly extinguished. A sudden disappearance of ego

[3] At least not unambiguously.

feeling of this nature is also found in narcolepsy. When the process of falling asleep is disturbed, the loss of ego feeling is only partial and gradual. . . . As long as a sleeper does not dream, he does not feel his ego. Whether an unconscious ego persists, or whether Friedrich Kraus's "basic personality" *(Tiefenperson)* corresponds to an ego or to the id, are still insoluble questions. It must be assumed that even in dreamless sleep, much psychic and even intellectual work, shrewd and intelligent arrangement and construction, takes place in the unconscious. Freud has compared the unconscious with the "good folk" in fairy tales who help us with our work during our sleep. But as far as we know, all the unconscious accomplishments during sleep are biologically centered through the unity of the body, and not psychologically through the unity of the ego. Hence Freud's statement that sleep is a narcissistic state refers to unconscious narcissistic cathexes which, if they are attached to any entity at all, at least are not attached to the ego of waking life. It is probable that Freud wished this statement merely to express in an extreme fashion the fact that with the exclusion of sensory stimuli, object cathexes are withdrawn to an incomparably greater degree than during waking life. The withdrawal of object cathexes permits narcissistic cathexes to become object cathexes, as when the person of the dreamer is wholly projected and appears in the dream as another person. Here, in our discussion of the manifest expression of narcissism in ego feeling, we must establish that in dreamless sleep this narcissistic cathexis of the ego is absent.

When, on falling asleep, consciousness is lost, ego libido ceases to be in the ego and all ego feeling disappears. It is mostly a matter of taste whether one says: that the ego libido vanishes *(versiegt)*, that it is asleep, that it is withdrawn into the id, or that it is distributed among the partial functions. However, this narcissistic cathexis always stands ready to return to the ego, as we see from the fact that except in pathological conditions, every stimulus which wakes the individual immediately re-establishes ego feeling.

In the *last* two sections, dealing with the "ego feeling" and the "significance" of its "variations in the dream" an attempt is made to supplement the findings of Freud concerning the "grammar" of the dream. "The different types of investment with ego feeling—either purely psychic ego feeling or psychic plus bodily ego feeling, active or passive, total or partial—express the various modalities of dream occurrences."

BELA MITTELMANN (*Ego Functions and Dreams,* Psa. Quart., XVIII, 1949) devotes himself to discussing "*the relation of dreams to the general integrative strength of the patient* in the analysis, his defense mechanisms, his self-evaluation and interpersonal attitudes, his anxieties, his concept of himself, and reality." The dream material is, as is much of the clinical material of this author, instructive. Two of the dreams and the interpreter's comments may be quoted here because they show him working on the same problem as Lionel Blitzsten and Ruth and Kurt Eissler (see pp. 115 ff.), and, in so doing, point to the growing interest of the analyst in the ego. In the author's own words: "The *functional strength* of the individual is estimated," in the case of these dreams, "by way of the relationship of the dream and its interpretability to the total analytic process. There are five types of such relationships. The functional strength of the individual, from the point of view of integration, is *highest* in the first example and *lowest* in the last." It is these two that shall here be transcribed.

First Example (highest "functional strength"). "The dream is clear, the patient accepts the interpretation and furnishes further relevant associations. This is illustrated by the dream pair of a fifty-year-old phobic woman.

"*Dream 1.* She is four or five years old and is about to make sexual advances to an idiot, a girl, in the lavatory, when the door opens and she stops with anxiety, shame, and guilt.

"*Dream 2*. Her mother is away from the house and she feels happy and free."

Author's Comment. "The patient related in connection with the dream that her mother caught her masturbating when she was five years old and severely shamed her. She could not stop masturbating, developed nightmares, the fear of being alone in the house, and clung to the mother. There was an idiot living in the house but, as she herself recognizes, the idiot in the dream represents the patient. She suffered from affective stupidity which resulted in difficulty in her school work. This was an attempt to deny responsibility for her sexual activity as well as for her hostility toward her mother who had shamed her. The hostility probably amounting to a death wish is indicated in the second dream. This, together with her constantly anticipated disapproval and condemnation by the mother, on whom she was helplessly dependent, increased her fear of abandonment."

Last Example (lowest "functional strength"). "The dream reveals some repressed attitude almost without disguise. The patient is deeply disturbed and the interpretation of the dream, often surmised by the patient, only adds to the distress. The patient may be on the brink of a psychosis. A thirty-year-old woman, suffering from asthma, after a year and a half of analysis during which she had made very good progress, had two dreams.

"*Dream 1*. She murdered her brother.

"*Dream 2*. She dreamed of a word 'flailure' which she immediately explains as being composed of 'failure' and 'flay,' both referring to the analysis."

Author's Comment. "The patient was restless and agitated, complained of feelings of strangeness and of passing thoughts of pushing people under subway trains. No attempt was made to analyze the dream. She was asked to sit up and face the analyst."

Reviewer: A few complementary observations may assist in evaluating the *method.*

In the *first* case the dream contains a memory; very likely one of seduction, either active or passive, which was traumatic because of its effect upon the castration complex of the phobic child. The associations and their interpretation are limited to the elaboration upon the trauma through compulsive masturbation, identification with the castrated female (ultimately the mother), and to the symptomatology ("fear of withdrawal of love"—Freud) indicative of the failure of elaboration. They do not touch, however, upon the repressed traumatic event, in whose stead a screen memory is related. This may be optimal for the analysis of the patient at that particular time; it is not so for the evaluation of her "general interpretive functional strength." The apparent "strength" is deceptive; because, on the one hand, the phobias, indicative as they are of "weakness" are cancelled by the "clinging" to the "mother" in the transference and because, on the other, the patient is not requested either to furnish more than a few spontaneous associations or to respond to a reconstructive approach to the trauma whose repressed memory is apparently contained in the dream. With regard to the method: the employment by Mittelmann of the reaction to dream interpretation as an indicator of the patient's "general integrative strength" is based upon an oversimplification, for it fails to account, among other things, for what is generally called the "depth" of the interpretation to which the reaction occurs.

In the *second* case the dream is indicative of an instinctual irruption *(Triebdurchbruch)* to which the ego, deprived of "asthmatic" instinctual discharge, responds with disintegration. This is not, however, the totality of the response, which includes a restitutive attempt. The fratricidal aggression of the first dream is displaced, in the second, upon the superego[4] and is, in analysis, either transferred or projected upon the analyst; erotized destruction (sexualized aggression, if you prefer) has thus found subject and object in the transference; narcissistic instinctual quantities have become object-libidinal, and "free" energy has been "bound." Although this integrative endeavor has failed to produce balanced economy, as is shown in the patient's anxiety and feelings of estrangement, it has, nevertheless, produced an association representative of the reconversion of a dreamed neologism into a waking expression of thought—an association, indicative of a tendency toward reintegration. The ego has thus responded to the irruption with a restitutive process, initiated in the second (part of the) dream and continued in the analytic situation. Since this spontaneous integrative attempt is abortive, an appreciation of the *"general* integrative functional strength" would require additional data about the degree to which the analyst was successful in stimulating its continuation. He could not, evidently establish the "beating fantasy," fundamental to the second dream or approach the inferiority feeling; but he might, for instance have succeeded in acquainting his patient with some clinical aspects of her sadomasochistic regression. Through having her sit up and face him, he assisted her toward extraversion; but we are not told either what he did beyond that or to what use, if any, she was able to put his assistance. It is data such as these that would have completed the report upon the quasi experiment, whatever its value, which the author had set out to conduct.

[4] A technique for turning aggression upon oneself. For the theory of the result, as developed by Freud, see pp. 135 f. of section "The Spoken Word."

VII.   THE EGO IN WAKING UP

PAUL FEDERN (*The Awakening of the Ego in Dreams,*
Int. J. Psa., XV, 1934) created the concept of "orthriogenesis," which requires examination because one finds it occasionally accepted. "It is probable that in sleep which is
entirely undisturbed the ego is without cathexis, i.e., is
cathected only as it is in an embryo (or perhaps we should
say: in a sleeping embryo). From such sleep the ego of the
day before awakes as the ego of the actual moment; the
more normal the sleep and the awakening, the more in-
stantaneous is the restoration of cathexis. It follows that
in a moment of time the ego has to recapitulate its whole
genesis. Since this phenomenon occurs daily with the coming of morning I propose to call it *orthriogenesis,* a word
coined on the analogy of *onto-* and *phylogenesis.*"

The reader in want of an opinion of his own may find
it useful to compare Freud's with Federn's remarks on the
subject. "What then is sleep?" Freud asks himself in the
fifth *Introductory Lecture*[5] and answers:

That is a physiological or biological problem concerning which much is still in dispute. We can come to no
decisive answer, but I think we may attempt to define
one psychological characteristic of sleep. Sleep is a condition in which I refuse to have anything to do with the
outer world and have withdrawn my interest from it. I
go to sleep by retreating from the outside world and
warding off the stimuli proceeding from it. . . . Thus the
biological object of sleep seems to be recuperation, its
psychological characteristic the suspension of interest in
the outer world. Our relationship with the world which
we entered so unwillingly seems to be endurable only
with intermission; hence we withdraw again periodically

[5] *A General Introduction to Psychoanalysis.* Garden City Publishing Co.,
Garden City, 1938, pp. 79-80.

into the condition prior to our entrance into the world: that is to say, into intra-uterine conditions—warmth, darkness and absence of stimulus—characteristic of that state. Some of us still roll ourselves tightly up into a ball resembling the intra-uterine position. It looks as if we grown-ups do not belong wholly to the world, but only by two-thirds; one-third of us has never yet been born at all. Every time we wake in the morning it is as if we were newly born. We do, in fact, speak of the condition of waking from sleep in these very words: we feel "as if we were newly born"—and in this we are probably quite mistaken in our idea of the general sensations of the new-born infant; it may be assumed on the contrary that it feels extremely uncomfortable. Again, in speaking of birth we speak of "seeing the light of day."

Freud, in other words, while producing the somewhat infelicitous formulation "Each awakening in the morning is then like a new birth"[6] criticizes the popular metaphor likening birth and arousal for its erroneous implication of an identity of sensations (*Allgemeingefühl*) of the new-born and the newly awakened. Thus he restricts the analogy between awakening and being born to the physiological precipitation of a psychological state of perceptiveness toward the outer world. With regard to the ego, there is, of course, no likeness between the two states: the erstwhile sleeper has a fully differentiated ego; the erstwhile fetus has none. Federn, however, elaborating in metapsychological terms upon Freud's semi-colloquial observation, defines the process of waking up as a matutinal reenactment of the ontogenetic repetition, constituting the first years of individual life, of the phylogenetic development of the species. Yet he does not report upon observations justifying this definition. The mere fact that when asleep without dreaming we have no ego and when awake we have one does not warrant terming the re-establishment

6 "Jedes Erwachen am Morgen ist dann wie eine neue Geburt."

of the ego after sleep a repetition of its establishment after birth.

With regard to the rest of the paper, the reader is asked to be critic; space available here does not permit opposing it, passage by passage, to the results of clinical observation or to the positings constituting the theory of the dream.

MARTIN GROTJAHN (*The Process of Awakening*, Psa. Rev., XXIX, 1942) attempts, in the main, metapsychological description of the process of waking up. The study provokes thought, is excessively inhomogeneous and, therefore, hardly suitable for abstraction; the author's treatment of his clinical observations is too fragmentary, his summary too extensive and his conclusions too often in need of corrective comment. Some of them have been reviewed and opposed to the fundamental ideas of Freud on the occasion of Jekels' and Federn's communications (cf. pp. 95 and 103) ; as for the rest, a good deal is rediscovery, some of it is obscure, some is incorrect, some controversial, some original and astute. One example of each and two of the last of these categories afford comment upon important points.

1. (Rediscovery): *Freud 1900:* "The fulfillment of the wish to sleep is as the well-known examples of the nurse's sleep, etc., show, quite compatible with the maintenance of a certain expenditure of attention in a certain direction." *Grotjahn 1942:* "The cognitive function of the Ego must remain awake in such cases (of training oneself to wake up at a given time) as that of the watchful mother who is awakened by the slightest movement of the baby. The same noise may not awaken the father who may, however, be awakened by a telephone call which, in turn, may not disturb the mother's sleep."

2. (Obscure): "The cognition of the inner mental reality

is apparent in the phenomenon of consciousness?" What, in the name of Aristotle and Freud, does this mean?

3. (Incorrect): "Only after the awakening of the volitional function may the influence of the Super-Ego become conscious (it works, however, unconsciously in the dream censorship)." Freud has in 1923 communicated the discovery that the superego—aside from whatever of it is continuously operative as "censor"—may occasionally be reestablished in the dream and radically affect its contents. The influence of the superego as distinct from that of the censor can, in other words, become conscious—perhaps better: affect consciousness—during sleep.

4. (Controversial): Silberer's much discussed "functional symbolism" is adopted uncritically by the author. "The gradual awakening of the Ego starts with a reconstruction of the intra-personal communication, is identical with the inner-cognitive function and appears in the form of 'functional symbols' (Silberer). These symbols differ from the dream symbols or material symbols in that they do not picture the content of the mind but how the mind is working." In the reviewer's opinion which he has not succeeded in either identifying with Freud's or finding it at variance (as far as he is able to ascertain, it was or became eventually that of Freud) there are no "functional" symbols. The misunderstanding arose, apparently, from the fact that falling asleep and waking up are, at times and in part, experienceable and therefore subject to thought. (So are of course other states during waking life such as, e.g., absorption in a work of art or concentration upon a scientific problem—which, after all, means no more than that at times one is able to be aware of what one is doing and to describe it.) Thought of this kind is, as is other thought, representable in the dream; and the dream work, in representing it, is assisted by allegorical and metaphorical concretizations. The state thus described and represented is

dream material. If it belongs to the past it is memory or day residue; if it belongs to the present, i.e., if the dream elaborates upon such a state while it prevails—as it does often with other states, physiological or psychological, such as ingestive or excretory needs, moods, etc.—it may precipitate a hallucinatory experience coincident with its occurrence. The result is in any case an overdetermination of a dream or a dream element otherwise indistinguishable from others. If the representation of such a condition, for example, of that of arousal, is an indirect one, it may naturally employ symbols; but the latter, when so employed, do not alter their meaning.

An amusing example, lacking symbolic representation, is presented by Grotjahn, as the "self-observation" of a person who actually succeeded in awakening at an intended time:

> I said to someone in the dream, "And now I have nothing else to do but turn my back on you with highest indignation." With that I turned slowly around on my heel, left my partner alone, and slowly, with an outspoken and clear feeling of indignation, opened my eyes and was awakened.

The dreamer—whom one is almost compelled to imagine as angry at having to wake up at a time, now "intended" but originally commanded—reinterprets, as Freud has expressed it, affects as well as state in the sense of a wish fulfillment: his anger becomes indignation, its object a someone to whom for once he is able to "give a piece of his mind." Thus, instead of complying reluctantly with an imposition upon his comfort, he disdains in the name of morality staying with the despicable companion of his dream, walks away in the grand manner and in so doing turns his back voluntarily upon sleep.

5. (Original): The same dream may perhaps demon-

strate a contention of Grotjahn's, which I do not remember having found elsewhere: "If bodily Ego feeling appears during the dream such as that observed during flying dreams or in the symbolic expression of eye movements, so the very beginning of awakening is announced. If the body is felt as a part of reality the decisive step in the process of awakening is performed." A dreamer turning slowly around on his heel, leaving his partner with outspoken deliberation and awakening may be presumed to experience a feeling of his body in the process of arousal. In Freud's "staircase dream" the feeling of bodily inhibition occurs likewise at the end, although it is not stated that the dream led to his waking up. The tenet requires clinical validation; were it found valid, it might add to the knowledge of the arousal dream.

6. (Original): The paper concludes with a small treatise so full of astute observation and so wisely economic of abstraction, that one cannot do justice to it except by quoting in full.

"ON BOREDOM"

A stage of Ego disintegration and Ego reconstruction may occur in stages of dullness and boredom. It is very significant that in the German language the word dullness is accompanied by the adjective 'deadly' to indicate a high degree of dullness. In English the expression is used 'bored to death.' It is quite true that dullness is an Ego danger because it is a stage of Ego starvation. The dull situation offers no opportunity to apply the cognitive or motor abilities of the Ego so that the Ego is put into a desperate situation of unemployment, faces a mental death and the result is a certain disintegration. Either the person actually drops off to sleep, thus ending the stage of real dullness and opening a stage of dreaming, or else he indulges in a stage of preconscious fantasy, now and again being interrupted by the demands of reality. A real enjoyment of fantasy is not possible—

the very nature of the dull situation does not allow the person to get away from reality but keeps him in a situation of frustrated expectation. This situation is connected with severe pain and therefore persons very often react with rather aggressive fantasies. It is quite apparent that in such stages of Ego starvation the person must unconsciously feel a masturbation temptation because the person's body is the only object which offers a possible occupation. In many of the mechanical activities of bored people we see a rather undisguised exhibition of masturbatory acts. They indulge in monotonous movements, rocking their chair, playing with a pencil, picking of the nose and so on. A very interesting experience of this mental stage during dullness may be found in the habit of doodling (which by the way is not confined to dull situations as every doodler knows). This document of human suffering has never found the interest of psychoanalysis to which it is surely entitled. It belongs to the few objective results of human activity which is performed without conscious Ego striving. It is automatic and remains, so to speak, unconscious even if performed. The majority of doodling persons do not recognize the authorship of their own products because they do not see the Ego features of their products. If persons could draw the symbols which they see during the process of awakening they probably would do so by drawing figures very similar to the doodling. The Ego level in dullness is similar to that during sleep. The temptation of dropping to sleep is inhibited by the authoritative character of the situation. Also because of lack of stimulation the application and use of the Ego functions is inhibited. The person lives through agonies of tension looking for outlets in dreamlike phantasies or in rhythmic activities.

The following reports are collected from the confessions of a number of psychiatrists after attending the same meeting. Most of the persons were analyzed:

Most of the questioned persons confessed that they tried to think their own thoughts, but that this was not possible. They always had to return to the speaker in order to realize again that it was impossible to listen to him. One person began to count the pictures on the wall. He got up to nearly 100 and then lost interest. Another person, without communicating with the first one, tried the same thing, then he thought he would like to shoot the pictures with a gun. Quite realistically he imagined how he would begin in the corner to his right and then go from picture to picture without leaving a single one out, always shooting in the face of the photographed person. A third one thought that he would die, then his soul would go through a keyhole with a loud whistling noise. Behind the door he would materialize again and enter his office. Still another person thought that he would try to get up in the air and remain suspended over the table, to the enormous shock and surprise of all those attending. Some persons could not remember what they had thought. Some of them were sure that they must have thought something but could remember only the sensation of pain and torture mixed with anger and the wish to protest. Nothing could satisfy them—neither swinging on their chairs, nor smoking, nor drawing. Some of these drawings were collected and are of extreme interest, showing compulsive mechanism, genital or anal symbolism—seldom the character of daydream illustrations. One person spoke about a phantasy which he had followed through different meetings: He thought that a man who was pictured in the biggest picture on the wall would come out of the picture and that it would have been very surprising to see a living man, but living only in the part which was pictured—namely, his head, a part of his chest, no arms yet with his hands holding a book. . . .

The reviewer has tried to account for his interest in this amusing report. If the state described in it is not, as the author has learned from the drawings, daydreaming proper, what is it? It is not out-and-out hypnagogic; but it appears that the characteristics that distinguish it from the daydream are. The situation, at once precipitative and inhibitive of either daydreaming or falling asleep, seems to occasion an unnamable, regressive state, indeed deserving of psychoanalytic attention.

VIII. THE NATURE OF SLEEP

LUDWIG JEKELS (*A Bioanalytic Contribution to the Problem of Sleep and Wakefulness,* Psa. Quart., XIV, 1945) attempts, as did others before him, to determine what sleep is. He circles the problem in a series of reflections worth following even if the pattern into which they are composed does not conform to that of one's own preconceptions. I, for one, am inclined toward doubting my competence to review his communication because the ratio of observable data to speculative elaboration is, in bioanalytic matters, the reverse of that to which the analyst is accustomed; the hypotheses are consequently, to borrow Freud's term, 'mythological," and better suited to being believed or disbelieved than reviewed. However, Jekels' argument is distinguished by moderation; he knows the physiologic and psychiatric literature well enough to quote it instructively; and he is so familiar with Freud's ideas that he is able to disown them where he chooses.

These are the salient points:

Freud's revolutionary conception that sleep is not merely a passive occurrence but an active process has been adopted by psychiatric and corroborated by physiologic investigators of sleep. Not "I fall asleep," one may sum it up, but "Je m'endore."

What is ascertainable about sleep from the dream is limited by the fact that the two coincide only at times. For there is dreamless sleep about whose nature dreaming cannot inform. Such, at least, was "Freud's opinion" and is "that of most analysts"; but it is not Jekels'. "Except in the case of sudden awakening through an external stimulus, *wherever there is sleep there is a dream.*" However, instead of deriving a conclusion as heavily fraught with implications as this from observations, the author merely refers to the "excellent studies on awakening by Silberer and particularly by Federn, Grotjahn and French." The reviewer remains unconvinced.

A problem: "In full sleep ego feeling is extinguished. . . . As long as the sleeper does not dream he does not feel his ego . . . [the] *narcissistic cathexis of the ego is absent in dreamless sleep.*" (Federn quoted by Jekels.) How, Jekels asks in effect, is this possible? Does not withdrawal of cathexis from the environment, upon which Freud had seen sleeping dependent, entail an *overcathexis of the ego?* Jekels' answer: "Freud's statement that the libido of the sleeping ego regresses to the stage of primitive narcissism is misleading; this is clearly a case of libido having been withdrawn from objects and flowing toward the ego—a state which Freud himself repeatedly, as for example in *The Ego and the Id,* designated as secondary narcissism. Apparently this kind of cathexis cannot wholly lose its character; it still bears traces of its origin and thus some connection with and dependence upon the object world. Small wonder therefore that during sleep, when the object world has become completely submerged, such a weak cathexis gradually fades out and finally vanishes entirely. The same thing happens to ego consciousness, or to quote Federn, ego feeling. Federn must have had a hunch of this situation since he mentions the extinction of ego feeling. . . ."

The reviewer is left confused. If, for argument's sake, he adopts the author's conviction that the sleeper is always dreaming, the problem no longer exists; because the dreamer, dreaming as Freud has expressed it, "in the last analysis always about himself," is without doubt excessively narcissistic. If on the other hand, he abides by his own conviction that the sleeper dreams but at times, the discussion lacks pertinence because "primitive narcissism" is essentially "primary" narcissism of which no mention is made.

"The loss of ego feeling is experienced as dying." (Federn quoted by Jekels from "Ego Feeling in Dreams," *Psa. Quart.*, I, 1932): "According to Freud, the ego is separated from the id; sleep means the temporary canceling of this separation. Metapsychologically, falling asleep initiates the return of the ego cathexis into the id. Phenomenologically no id can be observed; but one observes that the cathexis is lost and that one's ego returns to prenatal nonexistence." Jekels: "In contrast to Federn I am of the opinion that non-existence not only means a return to the prenatal stage, but also, at least to the same degree, a danger to the existence of the ego because this process—by which the ego and the personage (Kronfeld) are in sleep deprived of the specificity and reduced to a large extent to the uniform and undifferentiated state of the id or individual (Kronfeld)—is experienced as a mortal threat, as an *anticipation of death.*" Since the reviewer cannot, within the framework of this publication, present either data or argument in support of his disbelief, he must continue to confine himself to abstracting the views of the author: "The ego of the sleeper is about to perish, since in contrast to the schizophrenic it has been almost entirely depleted of libido." The sleeper is therefore capable of attempting "a normal resolution such as is actually realized in sleep"; while "the overwhelming narcissistic cathexis of the psychosis frustrates [an] attempt" such as, according to Jekels, was undertaken by Schreber, when he complemented his delusion of the end of the world with that of his own death.

Further *"evidence of how closely sleep and death are associated in the imagination of mankind"* is adduced (as it had been before in Bergler-Jekels' "Instinct Dualism in Dreams," cf. pp. 81 f.) from semantics, mythology, folklore. Dying, one enters "eternal sleep," sleeping deeply one sleeps "like the dead"; Hermes, bringer of sleep and dreams, is the escort of the dead to Hades; death and sleep were, in antiquity, but twin brothers. This, again, is no argument to the reviewer, who agrees with Freud that "the idea of death cannot be consummated [*ist unvollziehbar*]" and is, therefore, prepared to find that the idea substituted for it is both consolatory and illusive. . . .

"Why do we wake up at all?" Jekels' answer is predictable on the basis of his reported views: If sleep is a danger and the danger perceived as mortal it will precipitate counteraction. "The cognitive ego function, . . . which never vanishes during sleep, . . . concerned as it is with all parts of the personality such as the superego, the id, and the bodily ego, becomes aware of the impending threat to the collapsed bodily ego and therefore abruptly arranges for the process of awakening. . . . Having recognized voluntary withdrawal from the outside world as an active, dynamic element in the onset of sleep, we are consequently concerned with an *active* dynamic factor whose task it is, as it were, to prepare the ego in the process of awakening." The "cognitive function," the author explains, is Grotjahn's and French's; its existence agrees with Freud's statement that we know all the time that we sleep, and with the age-old observations of the proverbial sleep of the nurse and the miller. The function "works in two directions: the one as an inner or intrapersonal relation toward the mood of the person and the other as an interpersonal relation toward the outer world." (This idea is Freud's, who developed it in Section D of Chapter VII of *The Interpretation of Dreams;* Grotjahn's and French's is merely the language of current fashion.—Reviewer).

"There are two particularly striking elements" in the

restitution of the ego from sleep: first that it is effected by a "very intricate, unusually subtle mechanism. Secondly . . . ." that the latter "is to a large extent regulated by *the principle of time.* . . . in the sense" not so much "of simultaneity or of sequence but rather. . . . of tempo, i.e., of slow progress, of caution and careful avoidance of precipitate developments." Jekels quotes Grotjahn[7] who "found that a sleeper awakened suddenly by an external stimulus sometimes shows a reaction similar to that observed in people in the process of recovery after shock, namely, the total absence of the synthetic cognitive function." (For "absence" it should read "failure."—Reviewer.) And he concludes "that the slow and cautious progress of the process serves the purpose of preventing a possible traumatic effect from the intrapsychic perception of the danger threatening the bodily ego."

Dreams, in other words, have, according to Jekels (and others before him), an *"awakening function,"* which "constitutes their quintessence, their fundamental task." This function does not, he contends, conflict with their sleep-preserving function, nor does the conception of sleep as a quasi death contradict that of a return to prenatal existence. Return to the womb, preservation of sleep, restitution, follow the pleasure principle, while the "prehistoric" awakening function indicates to the author that we dream in the last analysis under the influence of the repetition compulsion, and that we do so in order to master the "traumatic" experience of sleep.

The ultimate nature of sleep? "Some periodically rotating process . . . recurring in daily oscillations" (Economo) to be identified "with the pattern of the almost incomprehensible cosmic process which produced life out of lifeless matter" (Jekels). "Sleep represents the repetition of by-

---

[7] M. Grotjahn and T. M. French, "The Process of Awakening," *Psa. Rev.,* XXIX, 1942.

gone forms of existence; even of the form of existence before the origin of life itself. And the awakening from it is
still caused by traumatizing forces which have awakened
the matter to life" (Ferenczi). The bibliographical matrix
of these presuppositions: ". . . . in the last resort it must
have been the evolution of our earth and its relation to
the sun that has left its imprint on the development of or-
ganisms. The conservative organic instincts have absorbed
every one of those enforced alterations in the course of
life and have stored them for repetition . . ." (Freud).

The reviewer remains more impressed by what Freud
has not said than by what his disciples are saying. "I have
had little cause to concern myself with the problem of
sleep," the author of *The Interpretation of Dreams* remarks introductorily on one of the first few pages, "for this
is essentially a physiological problem; although a characterization of the state of sleep must imply the alteration
of the conditions for the functioning of the psychic apparatus." If the problem is one of physiology we must wait
until physiology furnishes the solution. "Bioanalysis," is
not a science; it lacks a method; its tenets are the product
of divination. Those reported here appear untenable to
this reviewer.

The "wish to sleep" is epiphenomenal, as it were, to a
physiological alteration of the functioning of the brain,
quasi-instinctual and representative of a tendency toward
the quasi aim of a form of existence akin to that in the
womb. In going to sleep we fulfill this wish and we do
so with pleasure; after waking up we experience gratification. Having been pleasurably tired we are now pleasurably refreshed; in between lay a period of recreation which
it may be permissible to compare *in certain respects* to
the formative periods of fetus and youngest infant. If
entering upon it we are supposed to "anticipate death,"
has not the would-be sleeper been mistaken for an insom-

niac? . . . There are no observable data demanding or even justifying so radical an alteration of the fundaments of Freud's theory of the dream as the positing of an "awakening function." The arousal dream shows the sleeper resisting arousal; and, in studying the arousal dream, one gains in most instances the impression that arousal precipitates topographical reintegration rather than reintegration arousal. If there is no arousal stimulus, either external or internal—which, of course, may merely mean that none is demonstrable—the question "Why do we wake up?" must, as does the question "Why do we fall asleep?" await its answer from the physiologist; they are both complementary to the same physiological problem. Psychologically speaking there is, naturally, no reason why a gratification should not here, as it does everywhere, terminate the gratificatory performance (see also p. 112).

If sleep—and the object proper of physiology is, of course, dreamless sleep, not the partial wakefulness of the dreamer—produces, psychologically, extreme regression, we should certainly want to account for the accompanying defusion of instincts. (Its effects are even demonstrable in certain dreams.) But we cannot do so at present, either in the case of dreamless sleep or in that of the very young infant (where it might properly be termed nonfusion). It is the lack of topography that deprives us of all substrata for the description of cathectic processes or cathectic conditions; in the first instance because the topography has been relinquished in the course of regression, in the second because in the course of development it has not yet been established. In both cases we are faced with a situation such as that outlined by Freud (in the *New Introductory Lectures*) in his discourse upon the id. Confined to that situation we cannot observe analytically and gain material for legitimately speculative elaboration.

IX. THE HYPOTHESIS OF THE "DREAM SCREEN"

BERTRAM D. LEWIN (*Sleep, the Mouth and the Dream Screen*, Psa. Quart., XV, 1946; *Inferences from the Dream Screen*, Int. J. Psa., XXIX, 1948; *Mania and Sleep*, Psa. Quart., XVIII, 1949; and *The Psychoanalysis of Elation*, W. W. Norton, New York, 1950), has contributed more perhaps than any other author toward sustaining the current revival of interest in the dream. His work is much discussed and his concept, the "dream screen," adopted by some and rejected by others, has almost created factions. The controversy appears to concentrate upon the existence or nonexistence of this screen: and in doing so does, in this reviewer's opinion, an injustice to the author. The latter has, as I understand it, undertaken the task of pursuing the *process* of falling asleep into the *state* of being asleep and has established, what I would call a "tracer concept" for the purpose. The perceptory qualities of the "dream screen" are, therefore, of necessity self-canceling: dreamless sleep is a sleep in which nothing is dreamed but the screen; and the hallucinatory character of the screen is that of a "blank," causing sleep to be dreamless. It represents, in Lewin's opinion, the breast, whose incorporation he considers the aim of the wish to sleep and with which he believes the sleeper throughout to be "in unified contact." Is it not logical, then, to postulate that the dream, indicative as it is of disturbed sleep, contains both the screen, symptomatic of sleep, and the dream proper, symptomatic of the disturbance? "The intruding preconscious or unconscious wishes that threaten to wake the sleeper form the visual contents and lose their place in the sleeper's ego by being projected onto or before the dream screen." If the latter, as the author explains, is supposed to be "present in the dream though not necessarily seen . . . ."is it not a hypothetical concept and should it not be evaluated as such?

The value of a hypothesis derives from the need for it; and the need may depend upon the convictions of an investigator and the nature of the investigation.

Sleep [Lewin writes], *basically, comes from oral satisfaction. The baby after nursing falls into a presumably dreamless sleep. Theoretically it may be more correct to speak of the baby's having a "blank dream," a vision of uniform blankness which is a persistent afterimage of the breast.* Later in life, this blank picture of the flattened breast, preserved from the earliest experiences of nursing, persists in dreams as a sort of backdrop or projection screen, and like its cinematic analogue comes to have projected upon it the picture that we call the visual manifest content of the dream. The fulfillment of the wish to sleep produces only undisturbed sleep and the dream screen. *So far as falling asleep reproduces the infant's first sleep after nursing, it reproduces the fusion of the ego and the breast. The primitive sleeping ego is id, except for that dream screen, the erstwhile breast, sole and first representative of the environment. . . .*

I have italicized lest the reader, enjoying the almost colloquial ease of the author's style, overlook the conscientiousness of his formulations. Lewin's convictions are evident: in the first place, the "wish to sleep" need no longer retain the isolated position assigned to it by Freud, but is fully translatable into the terms of the theory of the libido. In the second place, there is a "primal dream," underlying all others, representative of the state of sleep and informative, psychologically, of its nature. It is in order to fathom this primal dream that he has fashioned the tracer hypothesis of the "dream screen."

The convictions are, of course, arguable; they are not, for instance, shared by the present reviewer who has intimated his standpoint on p. 108, and would maintain it here in spite of the fact that there it was expressed at the instance of a "bioanalytic" communication. It is true that Freud has eventually gone further. "One can rightly say," we read in his posthumously published *Outline*, "that at birth there arose an instinctual drive to return to the relinquished intrauterine life, a sleep instinct (*Schlaftrieb*). Sleep is such a return to the womb (*Mutterleib*)." But he has made no attempt to integrate this instinctual drive with his theory of the instincts. Calling its source somatic, its aim the return and its object the womb would be redundant; positing that it is sexual and its partial libido oral a speculation. The expectation, finally, of a basic dream, symptomatic of sleep and informative of the vicissitudes of the sleep instinct, does not, to this reviewer, appear either justifiable theoretically or fulfilled through a satisfactory demonstration.

With regard to the hallucinatory representatives of the "screen"—such as the author recognizes, for example, in the window of the primal-scene dream of the "Wolf-man," or in the paper of which an analyst dreamed that he was recording his dream—the reader will have to decide whether the similarity between concept and sensory product impresses him as one of form or of substance.

The reviewer—aware of the fact that there are dreams and dream elements distinguished through a relative or complete lack of depth dimension, as there are others characterized through its exaggeration—would not, nevertheless, either explain this, as does the author in terms of a "screen," or extend it into the average dream through the supposition of a "background." And the "blank dream" would still appear to him as one dreamed under too "high a pressure of the resistance" (Freud), with the result that dreaming is remembered, while the dream is not.

A hypothesis such as Lewin's should, however, perhaps

be judged solely by what its author achieved with its assistance. And the reader of Lewin's articles will not find them
wanting in astute observations. There is, for example, a
series of interesting dream interpretations, of which the
following is a characteristic instance:

> .... a patient, intellectually very coöperative, had been
> traditionally enjoined not to write down her dreams.
> Although she heeded my advice, her wish persisted. As a
> substitute gratification she dreamed of presenting me
> with a book printed in Braille characters, and that her
> breasts were bare while she was doing so. The book, of
> course was the record of her dreams. Freud's hint that a
> gift from a patient is a demand on the analyst, clarified
> the rest of the dream. *She wished the analyst to play the
> role of a mother and offer her the breast.*[8] In the trans-
> ference, this wish appeared as fantasies of borrowing or
> stealing my books to read at night before going to sleep.
> It will be noted that the dream screen gets separate rep-
> resentation in the dream, as a visually blank book; it is
> recognizable as the dream screen only by inference,
> from the fact of its being a blank "record" of dreams....

This interpretation, if incomplete because of an exclusive interest in the deepest determinant of the transference,
is flawless; and the "dream screen" is, as the author takes
care to explain, merely inferred.

There are other original contributions of general significance such as, for example, the interpretation of the
overflow of dream reports as symptomatic of a wish to sleep
in the analytic situation, and the technical suggestion to
interpret this to the patient in order to stop a particular
form of resistance.

There is an instructive discussion of Silberer's "functional" and "anagogic" phenomena, and of Freud's comments upon them which shows Lewin, in this reviewer's
opinion, as understanding Freud better than most previous

[8] The reviewer's italics.

writers except for Jones, on the subject. And there are, finally, various penetrating observations that caught the reviewer's interest when he first read them and continue to hold it upon rereading:

". . . the foetus with which the claustrophobe identifies himself is a retro-projected neonate and is supposed to be either eating or sleeping. The fantasy of returning to the mother's body is a secondary fantasy, combining the idea of union with the mother at the breast and later impressions. . . ." (This is true even if one favors Freud's opinion of the existence of a phylogenetic memory and believes that it contributes toward fantasies such as these.)

"From their dreams I learned that two depressed patients believed their skin symptoms were due to worms eating their dead body. They thereby identified themselves with dead mothers . . ." (The reviewer neglected to learn this in an otherwise thoroughly studied case of depression and has—consequently, he is inclined to believe—not succeeded in understanding one particular kind of recurrent skin lesions in his patient.)

"It is tempting to wonder, in passing, whether the mouth may not originally have been felt as a wound, so that the first healing attempt (to use the schizophrenic term) coincides with eating. . . ." ("Medicine"—one recalls in reading this—is homonymous for the science of healing and the remedy—in particular when the latter is taken by mouth.)

"Rado has correctly stated that the person who kills himself does not believe he is entering death, but immortality, the *paradis artificiel* of the addict's imagining. But there is another, an unwelcome immortality, as we know from the deathlessness, or extreme longevity, of the Wandering Jew, to whom it was a curse and a doom. Because he did not permit Christ bearing the Cross to rest in his shop this character had a rare penalty inflicted upon him: long life.

I suspect that this extraordinary sentence represents the 'immortality' of the sleepless, a bad case of insomnia. . . ." (It is not frequent that a problem—in this instance one of legend—appears solved completely through one single interpretation.)

X. DREAM ANALYSIS AND THE ANALYSIS OF THE EGO

N. LIONEL BLITZSTEN, RUTH S. EISSLER and K. R. EISSLER (*Emergence of Hidden Ego Tendencies During Dream Analysis*, Int. J. Psa., XXXI, 1950) contribute instructive clinical observations. With regard to their tenets, the first of them is a *technical* one. They deem Freud's advice against the patient's recording his dreams not consistently valid. "There are patients," they observe, "who are successful in counteracting their resistances by writing down their dreams. It is true that such dreams are always loaded with particularly heavy resistances and that the patient's need to write down his dreams must also be analysed. But under certain circumstances the written record may be an important contribution, and it may be of help to the analyst in steering the patient through a period of increased resistance by consistently providing him with a record of the patient's current dreams." If, upon occasion, an analyst feels assisted by such a record one is hardly entitled to say that he should not use it. Freud did; but he had the patient transcribe his dream only *after it had been recounted*. The reviewer, who has never found it necessary to deviate from this practice of Freud's, would be inclined to caution anyone but the most experienced against following the suggestion of the authors. As far as the analysis of the patient's need to write down his dreams is concerned, one should not forget Abraham's fundamen-

tal contribution to the subject. "A patient who brings notes
of a dream to the analytic hour wants unconsciously to
prove to the analyst by means of these notes that the dream
has particular reference to the latter."[9]

The second tenet is a *characterological* one. The production of associations by a patient to a dream resembles his
other productions; he associates as he does many other
things; it is the same "behavior" that he shows in analysis
and in life. The report illustrating this is as penetrating
as it is succinct:

> One of the authors had occasion to observe a patient,
> an obsessional character, whose technique of handling
> dreams distinctly repeated a basic pattern of his life
> history. His associations would go to a certain point and
> then he would drop the entire subject. His behavior in
> other pursuits followed the same pattern. He practised
> coitus interruptus in spite of having been advised against
> it. In his medical practice he changed to four different
> specialties one after the other. He had moved five times
> from one city to another in the course of his professional
> life. In the army he submitted obsequiously to his su-
> periors, only soon to become a source of such irritation
> that he was in danger of being court-martialled.

The third tenet, likewise characterological, extends the
second from the neurotic personality to the *psychotic*.
Patient I, "at least a borderline case," with "paranoid
mechanisms" and at one period "delusional ideas" has a
"reaction of panic and extreme rage which always occurred
whenever her attention was drawn to her dreams and she
was asked to associate to them. The violence of her objection was so great that she even sometimes jumped up from
the couch and huddled in the corner." She exhibited later
the same reaction when she had to show her artistic crea-

---

9 Karl Abraham, "Shall We Have the Patients Write Down Their
Dreams?" *The Psychoanalytic Reader*, I. International Universities Press,
New York, 1948, p. 328.

DREAM ANALYSIS AND EGO ANALYSIS 117

tions to an agent; but she presented it first in analysis and confined it there to the inspection of her dreams. Patient II, an erythrophobe with a "paranoid condition," begins her dream reports with "I had a peculiar dream" or ends them with "That's all there is to it." In so doing she produced her first "stereotyped" expression in analysis, and aroused the suspicion, confirmed subsequently, of a psychotic disturbance. With the first of these remarks she disavowed her dream; with the second she forestalled associations. It was not, however, the remark as such or its repetitiveness but the "voice" in which it was spoken, that initiated the diagnosis. In her daily life this patient opposed "criticism, and denied responsibility for any actions which were not ego-acceptable, just as she denied responsibility for her dreams." Patient III, diagnosis unstated, proved unanalyzable; "repetition, isolation and depersonalization became so strong that her treatment came to a complete standstill in spite of her continuous talking." But it began, again, with the dream. "Instead of associating . . . . she did nothing but repeat the manifest dream content in a stereotyped way without being fully aware of doing so"; as she had once done in school, when, reciting a poem, she reiterated the first verse instead of passing on to the second.

The authors believe that in each of these three instances "the patient's attitude during the process of dream analysis revealed an ego level which was effectively hidden in all other life situations." And they ask: ". . . . why did this hidden structure come to the fore just in the process of dream analysis? Is this due to personality peculiarities on the part of these patients, or is there perhaps something in the dream which provokes the waking ego when dealing with dreams to regress to an archaic, but still living, mode of dealing with the internal and external world? . . . What is that new structure which came to the fore in these clinical instances?" They state, finally, that "behaviour during dream analysis may become initially a particular source of information as to the degree of ego modification which might become revealed in the later course of analysis" and in so doing may be "a clinically important guide. . . ."

XI. A REMINDER CONCERNING THE METHOD

STEPHEN SCHOENBERGER (*A Dream of Descartes: Reflections on the Unconscious Determinants of the Sciences,* Int. J. Psa., XX, 1939) attempts the speculative interpretation of a dream and of its relations to the current preoccupation of the famous dreamer.

Freud, who had once been asked to interpret the very same dream,[10] considered it also replete with "waking thought" and declared it a "dream from above," i.e., one in which thoughts of the day are observable as disturbing sleep and whose interpretation is therefore particularly dependent upon elucidation by the dreamer himself. We —Freud explains in his miniature essay upon the subject—do not understand but the dreamer does; and he understands without difficulty because the dream's content is close to his conscious thought. "Our philosopher," he writes consequently to the French author who solicited his opinion, "does the interpreting and we are forced by all rules of interpretation to accept his explanations. But it is necessary to add that we ourselves have no way at our disposal that leads us to them." (". . . . que nous ne disposons pas d'une voie qui nous conduise au delà.") There is but little, therefore, that Freud can say; his scant comment upon the dream, expressive more often of question than answer, supplements Descartes' own but at two or

10 Freud, "Brief an Maxim Leroy, Ueber einen Traum des Cartesius," *Gesammelte Werke*, Vol. XIV, p. 558, Imago Publishing Co., Ltd., London.

three points. The place in it, indicative of an inner conflict, "hobbling," as Freud expressed it the interpreter-dreamer in moving freely among his own thoughts is perhaps worth quoting. The dreamer, trying desperately to enter a chapel in order to worship, meets two passers-by.

Il veut s'arrêter, leur parler; il remarque que l'un d'eux porte un melon. Mais un vent violent le repousse vers la chapelle.
   Il ouvre alors les yeux, tiraillé par une vive souffrance au côté gauche. Il ne sait s'il rêve ou s'il est éveillé. Mal éveillé, il se dit q'un mauvais génie a voulu le séduire et il murmure quelque prière, pour l'exorciser.
   Il se rendort.

It is the symbolization of "sinful" through the "left side," translatable independent of associations, to which Freud adds the somewhat cryptic interpretation of the wind as a representation of the "mauvais génie (animus)." And with regard to the melon, ununderstandable in itself, Descartes' idea that it is representative of the "charmes de la solitude, mais présentés par des sollicitations purement humaines" appears to Freud as an association from which an interpretation could, under ordinary conditions, be derived. For, if related to Descartes' state of sin, it might be looked upon as the pictorial form of a sexual representation which had occupied the young hermit's imagination.

That is all. With regard to the portraits Freud is even articulate about his lack of comment. "Sur les portraits," he finishes tersely, "Descartes ne donne aucun éclaircissement." In other words: if the dreamer is silent, we must be silent as well.

The reviewer, after studying Descartes' dream and Freud's comment, has asked himself whether he could go further, and has naturally found that he could. For instance, the nightmare part quoted above where the dreamer meets passers-by, one of whom carries a melon, and is pushed back by a violent wind toward the chapel, appears as a "primal scene" representation of the build of the "Wolf-man's" nightmare: copulative violence, represented there through its opposite, utter quiet, is represented here through allusion; the awakening of the child represented there indirectly, through the opening of the window, is represented here directly through the opening of the eyes, etc. However, such an example as this—one of several and easy to furnish—illustrates merely the well-known confinement of the unassisted interpreter to the elucidation of symbols or other typical representations. Add as one may to Freud's essay with such "translations," one does not augment its value, which is that of a diminutive treatise on method. M. Descartes is a human; that his dream is therefore a dream is a premise not a result. To proceed from this premise toward the result of the interpretation of an individual dream requires the dreamer's collaboration.

It is thus by the standards of method that the reader will have to judge the fourteen pages of Schoenberger's interpretation as compared to the two pages of Freud's. The reviewer desists because his competence is confined by the method.

In order to do justice to the author, and attenuate what may appear as intolerance on the part of the reviewer, it must be added that Schoenberger is aware of Freud's essay as well as of the speculative nature of his own observations. "Although Freud himself," he writes, "has remarked in connection with this dream that analysis of the dreams of historical figures offers little promise because we are compelled to dispense with the dreamer's associations, it was also Freud who showed us that, even when the material available is unsatisfactory and incomplete, it sometimes enables us to make constructions with useful results: only we must never forget the hypothetical character of these constructions. . . ." Furthermore, the reviewer is willing to admit his incompetence in still another respect: a biographer may consider a study productive of "useful results" if it shows him that his hero is made of the same stuff as we are; and that, collateral to his waking thought which has made him immortal, he thinks when asleep as do mortals.[11]

[11] J. O. Wisdom's "Three Dreams of Descartes" (Int. J. Psa., XXVIII, 1947, p. 11) is not a psychoanalytic study and is therefore not reviewed.

Part Four

GENERAL OBSERVATIONS

After reviewing so many different communications, written by different authors at different times, one is left with the feeling that a few general observations are in order. The first of these concerns the problem of translation, the second certain elements of the method of interpretation, and the third, the argument requisite to all emendation.

Since the Western centers of higher learning are today Anglo-American, a correct English *translation* of Freud is as urgently needed as is a complete one. This is, aside from the *Three Contributions to the Theory of Sex,* particularly true of *The Interpretation of Dreams.* The task is a difficult one; if it is unaccomplishable it is so not merely because Freud's syntax is frequently loose, and his style colloquially idiomatic, but because his relentless pursuance of unconscious expression has rendered the pun irreplaceable and the neologism resistant to substitution. Both pun and neologism, German or Viennese, are of course untranslatable; and so are, unfortunately, some of the indispensable terms. *Unerledigte Tagesgedanken,*[1] for instance, or *Mischbildung*[2] cannot be fully matched in English and

1 *Unerledigte Tagesgedanken:* Thoughts of the day that are not merely "unfinished" but have not been dealt with to the point of being ready to be dismissed, at least temporarily, after the fashion, as it were, of "that's that."

2 *Mischbildung:* The formation of a composite, e.g., of the image of two persons.

saying "womb" for *Mutterleib* in *Mutterleibsphantasie*[3] is substituting adult mentality for the mentality of the infant. Approximation, quotation, and circumlocution will have to suffice in replacing with an authentic text the work of the pioneer translator who was forced to transcribe one language into another without mastery of either. Since a competent English translation is at present being prepared abroad these remarks will become obsolete. They are made because they bear upon papers reviewed in this volume.

With regard to the *method of interpretation* it is difficult having read the literature, to refrain from repeating a few elementary rules "more honour'd in the breach than the observance," and to do so in spite of the fact that they *are* elementary and repeating them is repetitious. A dream is uninterpretable without *both* the analyst's and the dreamer's associations. The former betters the latter in the translation of symbols; the latter the former in the solution of allegory and metaphor, the elucidation of individual modes of expression, the identification of day residues, and the furnishing of historic material. The dream, "a communication," as Freud has termed it, "like any other," is, as are other communications, interpretable only in part, and at times. Associating to it, intentional in theory, is frequently unintentional in practice; the dreamer may, without either intent or awareness, associate to his dream. The latter will then, although it was not "analyzed," become understandable in a measure in the course of the analytic hour. However: only the intentional performance of the analysis of a dream by the analyst on the basis of the intentional furnishing of associations to virtually all parts or elements of it by the patient can be relatively exhaustive. One must, therefore, decide in the first place whether or not a particular dream should be ana-

[3] The fantasy of being or getting inside, or of returning into, the mother's "belly."

lyzed: if it should, it must be approached in one of the
several ways suggested by Freud and interpreted by the
rules of interpretation. (How much of this interpretation
should be communicated to the patient, and when, is a
separate problem.) The decision as to the analyzability of
a given dream rests on many grounds; the dreamer's ability
to "associate," and the relative "pressure of the resistance"
under which the dream was dreamed are but two. The
experienced analyst is often able to assess the potential
interpretability of a dream from its complexion. It is a
good rule of thumb, in the interest of interpretation as
well as of management, to refrain from dream analysis for
a varying period of time in the beginning of analytic
treatments.

With regard to a few particulars the following might be
profitably remembered: Confusion of *symbolism* with
allegory and *metaphor* is common. It is avoidable if their
disparities are remembered: the former is a mode of unconscious, the latter are two modes of preconscious, indirect representation; one inherited and the others acquired.
Symbolism is employed *by* the dream work, allegory and
metaphor are employed *for* it, i.e., in its service, because
they assist transformation of abstract thought into concrete
pictorial expression. The analyst holds the key to the symbol, the patient to allegory and metaphor; if the former
assumes the prerogative of the latter he is apt to replace
the dreamer's thought with his own.

Individual modes of expression are never altogether
symbolic; as far as they are, they are not individual but
representative of the occasional incidence of the symbol
in allegoric and metaphoric representation. Since these
modes are quite frequent, their occurrence alone should
justify the dependence of the interpreter upon the dreamer's associations.

With regard to *day residues* and *historic material* this

dependence is self-evident; perhaps the only day residue sometimes available to the analyst and unavailable to the patient is an element of a previous analytic hour, which in the dreamer had become (re-)repressed. (Historic material may, of course, by the same token, be remembered by the analyst and again forgotten by the patient.) The correct *establishment* of a day residue is not, however, equivalent to its *interpretation;* for the latter should show the residue as expressive of an ultimately infantile wish.

All in all, the interpreter must delineate for himself what he has not understood as sharply as what he has; Freud's terse remark at the end of his interpretative comment on Descartes' dream: "Sur les portraits Descartes ne donne aucun éclaircissement" should, in other words, be looked upon as *didactic*. If Descartes were a patient we would have to wait; if instead of waiting, we speculate, we would be apt to pursue our own thought, not his.

A remaining factor in interpretation, although I concede it reluctantly, is *intuition*. After subtraction of all that is method, this remainder is small; it consists, I believe, of a preconscious utilization of the totality of one's knowledge about species and individual as a frame of reference for the results of empathy with the latter. Using it wisely means in the first place remembering that one is not Freud; in the second, that intuitive interpretations should be kept to oneself until they are confirmable by applying the method. This is not, however, in all instances either feasible or economic; we are still, as Freud was, dependent upon supposal, and compelled by expediency to communicate suppositions occasionally ahead of their confirmation.

The abuse of "intuition" in interpretation will be reduced if the analyst learns to distinguish the particular factors of dream work prevalent in a given dream. Secondary elaboration—to mention one example—although ordinarily apt to inflate manifest content, may combine with condensation in producing a small dream or dream fragment of deceptive coherence. Only the preconception that the grammatical and syntactical elements of such a bit of dream text are not what they have become will induce the analyst to treat them for what they really are: fragments of different "spheres of thought" (*Gedankenkreise*) and focal points, therefore, for separate chains of associations. Thought—to mention another—that has resisted the transformation into visual images need not have resisted dreamwork. It may thus, for instance, form ruminative introductions or interpolations, sometimes long and excursive, while representative actually of a brief and simple pronouncement that holds the key to the rest, or a part of the rest, of the dream.

With respect to *addenda and emendations* it is the absence of proper argument in their support that requires a final comment. Freud's opinion on a disputed point is frequently not quoted at all, or if so, not fully; and the authors fail, in most cases, to show why it should be replaced. It is not demonstrated why old facts require new explanations or which new facts do; nor are divergent hypotheses tested by applying them to the original observations of Freud. The writers enlarge upon Freud's abstractions without examining them and confute his tenets without either proving or at least making it probable that they are false. If, for instance, the dream has an "awakening function," Freud's interpretation of the "Dream of the Burning Child" is not only in error and must be corrected but the fundamental deductions from it must be shown as dispensable in the theory of the dream. If a "basic dream" is observable and informative of the nature of sleep, Freud was wrong in dismissing the problem of sleep as physiologic; his opinion must be shown as based on deceptive evidence, and at least some of the errors in the theory of the dream, unavoidable on the basis of so erroneous a premise, must be exposed. If an interpreter of the dream of Descartes borrows a multiple of what Freud has borrowed from general analytic knowledge must he not name his collateral? Is he not under the obligation to present a set of facts, hitherto either unknown or unappreciated, or a method, hitherto unemployed, that enables him to dispense with the dreamer's associations?

Of the so-called "dissenters," whose publications are not included in this review, one would not expect an awareness of such an obligation; if they had it, they would not have dissented. Of the analysts, to whose work this review is devoted, one must remember that their training is medical and that there has been little time to outgrow it. Medicine, drawing upon the sciences, is not itself one; its approach to science is pragmatical, its tradition eclectic. Psychoanalysis, however young, is a science; it shares, therefore, with other sciences, certain fundamentals whose study will at a future time likely initiate psychoanalytic education. A preliminary instruction in logic and epistemology would, for instance, enable the analyst to apply to his field general indispensable principles of method.

As for the analyst of today, no one could now maintain—as Freud did two decades ago—that he "acts as though he had nothing to say" to the dream; even a cursory glance at the table of contents of the present volume shows a wealth of subordinate subjects and proves that interest in the dream has been revived.

Part Five

R. F.: ON THE "SPOKEN WORD" IN THE DREAM

In the *Bulletin of the American Psychoanalytic Association* (V, 1949, 40) Robert Waelder reports briefly upon a symposium to which Otto Isakower contributed the "appealing hypothesis" that since "the nucleus of the superego is auditory . . . . words in a dream may be a contribution of the superego to the dream."

The hypothesis is appealing indeed. The present writer —intrigued to the point of devoting research toward its clinical validation and the establishment of a theory for it—found that it bears, however, upon an excessively intricate subject. Freud himself has contributed to this subject more than is commonly known. In assembling his contributions by way of an exposition they call for some sort of classification and are perhaps best presented under three different headings:

I. DIRECT SPEECH IN THE DREAM[1]

The problem has been treated twice: In 1900 in *The Interpretation of Dreams,* and in 1916 in "Metapsychological Supplement to the Theory of Dreams." In the first of these sources the dream speech is, initially in the fifth

[1] In view of the lack of an adequate English translation of *Die Traumdeutung* the references are to the original; the translations are this writer's.

chapter, recognized as (1) a product for which the raw material can be found in the waking life of the dreamer. This raw material, however, is not only fragmented,[2] slightly altered, and deprived of its content in order to yield the product, but it may also be subjected to a process of selection. If it is, the speech, by virtue of a displacement appears in the dream instead of another speech. It is the latter that should have entered the dream, it is the former that did. Both were associated in waking life; the one excluded from entry into the dream must, in analysis, be separately recalled and interpretatively put in the place of the other if the thought expressed through the "spoken word" is to be understood. Freud's example: the "I do not know that" in the "Butcher dream." The dreamer, he writes, "had on the preceding day said this to her cook with whom she had had a quarrel, but had added: 'Behave decently.' . . . Of the two phrases . . . . she had taken the meaningless one into the dream; but only the suppressed one . . . . tallies with the rest of the dream content." We may amplify: only the suppressed one, the imperative admonition, is an utterance easily traceable to the superego.

In the sixth chapter a comprehensive formulation is rendered which contains six further tenets to be added to the one abstracted above:

(2) Dream speeches are definable as "speeches in the dream that own something of the sensory character of speech and are described by the dreamer as 'speeches.' " They are "felt to be quasi heard or said"; i.e., they own an "acoustic or a motor emphasis collateral to their occurrence in the dream" ("akustische oder motorische Mitbetonung im Traum"[3]).

---

[2] *Die Traumdeutung.* Imago Publishing Co., London, pp. 309f. (Vol. II-III, *Gesammelte Werke*) .

[3] *Ibid.,* p. 422.

(3) When conspicuously prominent as a speech the dream speech is reducible to a speech spoken or heard in reality by the dreamer. When not so prominent, "reading matter is apparently for the dream material in the dream a source that flows abundantly but is difficult to pursue."[4] (The first of these tenets is assertive; the second suppositional and refutable on the basis of Freud's own report and the analysis of the dream "Non vixit.")

(4) The dream speech may be fragmentary and its coherence deceptive; under analysis it may fall apart and reveal that the "raw material," besides having been broken up in the manner described above, has also been joined anew. Thus the "product," the speech in the dream, although containing the words, does not contain the meaning of the speech in the waking life.[5]

(5) Close inspection shows the dream speech to be composed of two kinds of elements: one "thorough and compact" and the other merely holding the first together after having been supplied in the manner in which a reader will substitute letters and syllables for omissions.[6]

Intermediarily in another place in the sixth chapter, Freud adds that

(6) the dream speech need not be meaningful in itself but may instead be merely allusive to an event coincident with the speech in waking life.[7] At the same time he clarifies, although indirectly, an important point: the speech in waking life must

(7) be conscious in order to be reproduced in the dream. A single event to the contrary—the reproduction of unconscious compulsive thoughts in a dream speech—is termed by him an "exception."[8]

4 *Ibid.*, pp. 422f.
5 *Ibid.*, p. 422.
6 *Ibid.*, p. 422.
7 *Ibid.*, p. 310.
8 *Ibid.*, pp. 310 ff.

The synopsis rendered here leaves no doubt that the raw material, in order to yield the product, may be subjected to every phase of the dream work—displacement, condensation and secondary elaboration.

In the second of the sources named previously, "Metapsychological Supplement," the dream speech is treated in a few lines whose quotation may precede comment: "Only where the verbal ideas in the day-residues are recent, actual fragments of perceptions, and not the expression of thoughts, are they treated like concrete ideas, becoming subject to the influence of condensation and displacement. Hence the rule laid down in the *Traumdeutung,* and since confirmed beyond all doubt, that words and speeches in the dream content are not new formations, but are imitated from speeches from the day preceding the dream (or from other recent impressions, such as from something read). It is very remarkable how little the dream-work adheres to verbal ideas; it is always ready to exchange one word for another till it finds the expression most favourable for plastic representation."[9]

The passage includes the following tenets:

(8) The raw material is a day residue: the speech in waking life was either spoken, heard, read or thought on the day before it is reproduced as a dream speech.

(9) The principle guiding the dream work on a speech in the dream is the regard for plastic representation.

(10) For the purposes of the dream speech the dreamer treats verbal day residues in the manner not of a dreamer but of a schizophrenic: a word image in the speech of the day before is not conceived as representative of a thought element or of an object but as an object itself. It is not, therefore, reduced to the object image denoted by it, but

9 (1916), "Metapsychological Supplement to the Theory of Dreams," *Collected Papers,* IV, pp. 143-144. Hogarth Press, London, 1925.

it is instead, as are object images, subjected directly to displacement and condensation. The dream work does not, in other words, deal with the word as intermediary between thought and idea but as idea; it does not succeed in laying hold of the idea represented verbally but it seizes upon and exhausts itself on the word.

In opposing the tenth to the first of the tenets formulated above a contradiction becomes apparent: descriptively Freud had termed the alteration of the waking speech "slight"; metapsychologically he implies that it is drastic. Clinical observation shows actually about all imaginable degrees of alteration; from the unaltered or slightly altered to the neologistic speech in the dream. Resolving this contradiction means enlarging upon one factor, formative of the dream and of the dream speech: secondary elaboration. The latter is implied as at work in its ordinary form in the fifth tenet where the speech fragments are described as joined through essentially meaningless verbal elements whose only purpose is to hold these fragments together. However, there seems to be another form of secondary elaboration operative in the unaltered speech. Here the dreamer, taking advantage of the fact that the speech had been conscious in waking life and has consequently already been elaborated upon secondarily, quotes it verbatim. He employs it, in other words, not as raw material, to be taken apart and rebuilt, but as finished product; and in so doing saves himself the task of secondary elaboration. This form has not hitherto been described. It proves naturally, as does all secondary elaboration, indistinguishable from wakeful thinking, and resembles therefore an ordinary quotation, inserted because it eliminates the effort of expressing a thought anew or the risk of expressing it less precisely. A dreamer, to give an example, sees a recumbent nude woman who says to him: "I have no milk." He has difficulty in identifying the speech, although he had heard it but shortly before retiring when his wife upon opening the ice-box and noticing that there was no milk had spoken these very words. The analysis proves the woman the mother of whom it had been said that she had no milk and therefore could not breast-feed her children. Needless to add that this speech is in the dream expressive of self-observation and thereby, if Freud's topographical allocation of this function be accepted, of a thought issuing from the superego.

In the present context the tenth tenet is the most significant one. For the lack of topographical regression to visual object representations in the formation of dream speech does not imply a lack of historic regression. Since the earliest word images are however, acoustic, the percepts—selected, fragmented, displaced, condensed and rejoined—have their origin in the auditory sensory sphere. They should, therefore, if this sphere is its nucleus, be contributed by the superego.

II. AUDITORY PERCEPTION—THE ORIGIN OF THE SUPEREGO

The description of auditory perception as the origin of the superego is Freud's. His formulation is the first and, as of today, still the most comprehensive because it accounts simultaneously for superego, ego, and id. In attempting a sensory allocation of the superego he remains aware that the latter is, by virtue of its definition, partly ego and partly id; and in assigning its origin to "word remainders," i.e., acoustic memory traces of words, he remembers that this sensory territory had already been occupied by the ego. Thus the superego, when any of it becomes conscious, appears joined auditorily to the ego; while it remains when unconscious, as does all id, indescribable except in terms of cathectic energy without known substratum. It is, Freud writes, with "regard to the importance we have ascribed to preconscious verbal residues in the ego, that the question arises whether the superego, if it is in part unconscious, can consist in such verbal images, or, if not, in what it does consist. Our answer, though it does not carry us very far, will be that it cannot possibly be disputed that the superego, no less than the ego, is derived from auditory impressions; it is part of the ego and remains to a great extent accessible to consciousness by way of these verbal images (concepts, abstractions); but the cathectic energy of these elements of the superego does not originate from the auditory perceptions, instruction, reading, etc., but from sources in the id."[10]

It is evident, on the basis of this description, that a speech contributed to the dream by the superego is also expressive of ego; and that a theory of the dream speech must fail if it disregards this overdetermination.

III. SUPEREGO AND DREAM

To this subject Freud has again contributed twice. The first of his contributions is known to everyone, while the second has hitherto found but little attention.

(1) The superego is reduced in the dream to a single one of its functions and identifiable as the "censor," described originally in *The Interpretation of Dreams*.[11]

(2) The superego, shrunk disintegratively to a mere censor, may in the dream expand reintegratively to the extent of being re-established completely. This occurs, as Freud has stated in his "Remarks upon the Theory and

10 (1923), *The Ego and the Id*. Hogarth Press, London, 1927, p. 76.
11 p. 149.

Practice of Dream-Interpretation,"[12] when the dreamer's attempt toward an unconscious infantile wish fulfillment has the effect of invoking the superego against it. The dreamer, who complies ordinarily with the censor by modifying the wish, complies in this instance with the superego by replacing it with a reaction formation. He excludes thus the original wish from the dream and with it much latent thought from the manifest content. But he does not furnish us with an exception to the wish-fulfilling tendency of the dream. For he supplants the dream wish with the wish for punishment; and in so doing exchanges merely one form of gratification for another.

Freud had formulated a theory of the punishment dream once before in *The Interpretation of Dreams:* "It would then remain the essential characteristic of punishment dreams that the dream-forming element *(Traumbildner)* is here not the unconscious wish from the repressed (the system Ucs) but the wish for punishment. The latter is a reaction against the former and, although unconscious (i.e., preconscious), belongs to the ego."[13] He has later added a footnote to this formulation designating it as the "point for the insertion of the superego. . . ." It is impossible at the present time to perform the task of reconciling the two formulations completely or of correcting the first one so as to yield the second. All one can do is to assume that the re-establishment of the superego causes—as does its establishment—both a defusion of instincts and a redistribution of instinctual energy, collateral to the topographical differentiation. "There are two paths," Freud wrote in the same year in which he advanced the re-establishment of the superego in the dreamer, "by which the content of the id can penetrate into the ego. The one is direct, the other leads by way of the ego-ideal; which of

[12] (1923), *Collected Papers,* V. Hogarth Press, 1950.
[13] *Die Traumdeutung,* p. 564.

these two paths they take may, for many mental activities, be of decisive importance."[14] It appears that dream and punishment dream are a case in question. In both it is the id upon which the ego draws for the wish; in the first instance altogether directly, in the second in part indirectly via the superego. Were this not so, Freud's formulation, quoted above, of the distinction between dream wish and wish for punishment would remain meaningful only if one were to assume that the exchange of one for the other is coincident with an exchange of superego for ego. It would then be the superego alone that experiences gratification at the expense of and in contradistinction to the ego; and the "dream-forming" wish for punishment would have to be understood as a wish of the superego to punish instead of a wish of the ego to be punished by a punitive superego. It is not, however, so understood. "The need for punishment," Freud has defined, "as an instinctual utterance of the ego which under the influence of the sadistic superego has become masochistic, i.e., employs parts of an instinctual drive towards inner destruction, extant in it for an erotic attachment to the superego."[15] It is, in fact, this masochistic compliance that enables the ego to preserve sleep through dreaming instead of undergoing arousal—the alternative, designated by Freud, in the case of objection by the re-established superego to a dream.

To these two instances of re-establishment of the superego in the dream the hallucination of speech can now be added as the third. Its kinship to the first instance becomes evident when the speech is critical or expressive of condemnation; to the second, when it precedes or accompanies an arousal. In either instance, the spoken word is a result of the interaction of superego and ego and will therefore

14 *The Ego and the Id*, op. cit.
15 (1930), *Civilization and Its Discontents*, Chap. VIII. Hogarth Press, London, 1946.

have to be understood as engendered jointly by both of these institutions.

*

In investigating a subject as complex as the spoken word in the dream it is advisable to proceed by the smallest steps, to take one at a time and, by retracing them, to make certain that one has remained on solid ground. The ten tenets, abstracted above from Freud's theory of the dream speech under the first heading, shall therefore be examined and amplified separately in the light of those abstracted under the second and third (see pp. 133 ff.).

Naturally, if a speech in the dream is dependent upon a re-establishment of the superego, the thought expressed in the speech must reflect not only the critical and the punitive function of the institution but on occasion its other functions as well.[16] Many a dream speech that seems at variance with the tenet befits it, if the different functions of the superego are kept in mind. A self-observative speech has already been quoted.

Ad (1) *Fragmentation, alteration, and selection*

The speech "I do not know that" in the "Butcher dream,[17] expressive in Freud's terminology of a "defensive objection," *(abwehrender Widerspruch)*, is, I believe, representative of such a further function of the superego: the instigating of repression. In so being it is, of course, simultaneously expressive of the compliance on the part of the ego; for the latter having repressed, reacts, as is affirmed in

16 Cf. Waelder's comment *(loc. cit.)* asking "whether the superego that may be responsible for the verbal rests which remain in the general retreat to the pre-verbal stage is meant only in the sense of conscience or also in the broader sense of self-observation and self-objectivation."

17 *Die Traumdeutung,* pp. 189 f. and 423.

the speech, to the re-emerging memory of the seducer's exhibitive offer with a typical *jamais vu*.[18]

Ad (2) *Sensory character of and description by dreamer as "speech"*

If the *thought* expressed in the dream speech is representative of a superego contribution, the contribution is one to the *second* phase of the formation of the dream, where an unconscious tendency, expressing itself in preconscious day residues, becomes preconscious itself. If the *"acoustic or motor co-emphasis"* characterizing the speech reflects likewise a contribution of the superego it is one to the *third* phase of the dream formation productive of the hallucinatory effect.[19] In other words, the superego contributes twice: once dream material, once hallucinatory distinction; once the thought to be verbalized, once the verbalization. Both contributions are made in collaboration with the ego; of the first this has been discussed, of the second it is implied by Freud through the equivalence of acoustic and motor characteristics in his definition of direct speech in the dream. While the acoustic qualities are in part traceable to the superego, the (speech-)motor qualities are not; they are symptomatic of the participation of the ego. One, however, does not characterize the dream speech any more or less conclusively than the other. (The nonregressive analogon is, of course, the direct speech in fiction. It is set off punctuatively from the text conveying scene or scenery, action or rumination, and is intended to be read, if silently with different acoustic, if aloud with dif-

18 The analysis, omitted by Freud, of the second part of the speech, confirms this instructively; but is performable only in the language in which it was spoken. The sentence is, furthermore, in its predicate, assonant to the suppressed sentence from waking life which finds thereby at least an allusive representation in the dream. ("Das *nehme* ich nicht"— "*Benehme*n Sie sich anständig.")

19 For an abstract of Freud's description of these phases (in "Metapsychological Supplement to the Theory of Dreams") see pp. 133 ff.

ferent motor qualities, imitative in either case of the speaker.)

Ad (3) Spoken or heard vs. read

The distinction is an untenable one. Freud was not clear on the point; the speech "Non vixit,"[20] for instance, is extremely prominent and experienced as spoken in the dream ("But I *say* . . . : Non vixit"); yet it stems from reading matter during the day. His confusion becomes evident when he "recalls : . . . that the two words had owned such a high degree of distinctness in the dream, not as being heard or exclaimed but as being seen,"[21] while the report on the dream is unambiguous in that they had been exclaimed. The contradiction is the result of a replacement of the actual with the potential day residue and, thereby, of the memory of the motor and sensory qualities of the dream speech with those of the speech from the waking life of the dreamer.

The exigency compelling such transformation of the spoken into the written word cannot here be examined; but it need be acknowledged that the most general characteristic of speech in the dream is that it is *direct* speech. This characteristic is constant and it is sufficient; the sensory qualities of the spoken word discussed in the preceding paragraph are inconstant and may even be absent. If the speech is neither spoken nor heard but is instead, as Freud has expressed it, "remembered vividly,"[22] it represents, as we have become accustomed to calling it, a "verbal" dream part; or, if the rest of the dream is forgotten, a "verbal dream."

20 *Die Traumdeutung*, p. 424.
21 *Ibid.*, p. 425.
22 *Ibid.*, pp. 304-305.

Ad (4) Broken-up day residue joined anew; meaning of dream speech different from waking speech

This describes a phase of the dream work illustrable with the nonverbal beginning of the Butcher dream.[23] Freud's patient had two separate experiences while awake: being late for the market and having a fight with the cook. In the dream they are joined: "She goes to the market with her cook who carried the basket."

With regard to the difference in meaning of dream speech and waking speech it is possible, under conditions of insufficient familiarity with the subject, to confuse the two when the latter is also traceable to the superego. The confusion is of the same order as that discussed by Freud between dream wish and day residue when the latter is also expressive of a wish. In both cases the day residues are, as they are always, merely dream material.

Ad (5) Two kinds of elements in the dream speech

The second kind corresponds to the Kittgedanken (binding thoughts?)[24] described by Freud elsewhere in The Interpretation of Dreams, and is, as they are, a product of secondary elaboration. The absence of this kind of element is characteristic of the particular type of secondary elaboration described above (cf. pp. 132 f.).

Ad (6) Meaningless dream speech merely allusive to an event

The present writer has not succeeded in either validating or invalidating this—theoretically improbable—tenet, of which Freud fails to furnish an illustration.

Ad (7) The model speech in waking life must be conscious

The occasional reproduction of unconscious compulsive

23 Cf. above.
24 Ibid., p. 494.

thought is termed by Freud an exception.[25] Compulsive thought, however, is frequent, and so is the unconscious nature of much or of most of it. Is it only exceptionally reproduced in a speech in the dream? I am unable to furnish the answer which, in view of the prominent participation of the superego in the formation of compulsive thought, should be instructive.

Ad (8) *The dream speech is a day residue*

The speech reproduced in the dream has occurred on the day before; it shares thus in the ultimate qualification of the day residue, perhaps not as yet completely understood, that one "has not slept over it" before dreaming.[26] The inconstancy of the sensory qualities of the "product" (cf. *ad* 3) furthermore corresponds to that of the "raw material." The speech from waking life may, in other words, be either heard, spoken or read; it need not, however, as does the "spoken word" in the dream, be "direct" speech.

Ad (9) *Dream work conditioned by regard for plastic representation*

The tenet requires amplification. The regard for plastic representation is in the case of the spoken word, as it is generally, but one factor conditioning the dream work; the other is the *compliance with the demands of the censor.* Either of them may prevail, either be absent. This is a clinical observation, easily verifiable through the analysis of many a speech in the dream, which surprises at first because it seems to suggest that the superego censors itself. Upon second thought one recalls that the speech is contributed jointly by superego and ego and that one should therefore expect it to be censored upon occasion. If, for instance, "Behave decently," the material for the speech in the Butcher-dream,[27] were merely an admonition

25 Cf. above.
26 *Ibid.*, pp. 187 f.
27 Cf. above.

of the dreamer by her superego, as it had been one of the maid by the future dreamer, it would have been eligible for entry into the dream. But it is not merely an admonition by the superego; it is also part of a fantasy of the ego concerning a sexual provocation by the parental figure of Dr. Freud. "It would," he wrote, "have befitted the phantasy underlying the dream very well; but it would at the same time have betrayed it."[28] The demand that it remain in repression and be not betrayed in the dream is a demand of the censor. The latter, undeceived by the dreamer's rejection of the attack under the dictates of her superego, is aware that she fantasies and therefore wishes it in the first place.[29] Its representation, even indirectly through an allusion implying it, is consequently impermissible and the censor demands additional dream work. The result: the allusion to the fantasy by the speech is replaced through that to the speech by another speech. This allusion, although twofold—once on the basis of juxtaposition and once of assonance—is both times remote enough to fulfill the requirements of the censor.

To sum up: it is the ego that fantasies under the impulsion of the return of the repressed from a time when there had not yet been a superego; it is the superego that enters the fantasy in a speech expressing rejection. It is the ego that dreams and speaks in the dream; it is the superego that, permanent and rudimentary as a censor, requires dream work on the speech and, temporarily re-established, enforces "direct speech." Thus the speech "I do not know that" is paradigmatic for the *ambiguity of the spoken word in the dream*. It is allusive, simultaneously, to a fantasy reproductive of an infantile trauma and thereby expressive of ego, and to an element in the fantasy reactive

28 *Die Traumdeutung*, p. 423.
29 In simple language: "The lady doth," as does the Player Queen, "protest too much . . ." (*Hamlet*, III, 2) .

to it in terms of the conscience and thereby expressive of
the superego. One could say that it is the ego that speaks
and the superego that makes it speak and, in applying
Freud's formulation, suppose that in the first instance content of the id penetrates into the ego directly, in the second, by way of the ego ideal.

Ad (10) *"Schizophrenic" treatment of word images from
    day residue which are subjected to dream work as
    though they were objects*

The paradigm for such treatment is the neologistic
dream speech, identical with the neologistic speech of the
schizophrenic.[30] We will supplement Freud's analysis of a
speech of this kind, in order to illustrate the significance
for the spoken word in the dream of the superego as the
carrier of the ego ideal. The illustration may, however, remain unconvincing unless it is considered in the light of
the general theory developed further below (pp. 145 ff.).

The dream,[31] one of Freud's own, is in its second part
a "verbal dream" consisting of the neologism *Autodidasker,* upon which the first part furnishes comment in terms
of a brief fantasy, formed several days before and "inserted" into the dream: Freud is telling Professor N. that
the patient seen last by him as a consultant suffers really—
against Freud's expectation and in accordance with N.'s—
only from a neurosis; in other words, that Professor N.
had been right and Freud wrong.

The neologism falls apart, associatively, into three fragments: *Autor* (author)—*Autodidact*—*Lasker.* The reader
familiar with Freud's analysis[32] may have noticed that it

[30] For a neologistic verbal dream in a psychotic, see p. 92. It epitomizes
the twofold origin of the "spoken word" and qualifies, through the obvious presence of a sadomasochistic relation between ego and superego
(analyst and patient in the transference) , as a close relative of the punishment dream.

[31] *Die Traumdeutung,* p. 304.

[32] *Ibid.,* pp. 305 ff.

centers around the third fragment and that the other two are interpreted only as reiterative of the third; the second, in particular, figures merely as allusive through the opposite and thus as expressive of the idea that education averts certain dangers incurred in associating with women.

A supplement to the analysis of the dream speech must therefore establish the chief determinant of "author" and "autodidact" by means of a more thorough exploitation of the scanty material.

The alternative right or wrong, representative of the critical judgment correct or incorrect, suggests the participation of a superego that in the scientist has replaced its originally moral standards while at the same time becoming more severe and more absolutistic; there is no venial error in science and no secession. The episode with the patient, however, which if looked upon as an incident proved N. right and Freud wrong, proves Freud right and N. wrong, if it is looked upon as a crucial experiment at a juncture in psychiatric thought. According to Freud's new science, of which he was the only exponent and to which N. was opposed, there should not have been a neurosis without sexual etiology and there had actually not been one; the neurosis was present but so was the etiology, which the patient had merely concealed. In other words, the "author-autodidact" had been proved an "N." Had this been the case of a younger man who, by mastering a craft, obtains the approval of an older one representative of it, it would in the realm of narcissism have been that of a filial ego satisfying its superego, incarnation of the parental demands. But it was not such a case. It was the case of an innovator who discards these demands, supplants them with his own, and is consequently alone, as it were, with his subject. Instead of pleasing his father he can therefore only attain his "ideal." That in doing so he elaborates nevertheless in the last analysis upon Diderot's "petit sauvage qui . . . . tordrait le cou à son père et coucherait avec sa mère"[33] becomes apparent in his associations to "Lasker."

It is necessary, in the interest of a metapsychological clarification, to designate the subject of these originally oedipal strivings, and convenient to reserve for it the term *ideal ego*.[34] Their gratification, in the present instance under conditions of sublimation, is particularly dependent upon the relation of this early subject (ego) to the later ideal (superego).

The general ambiguity of the spoken word, representative generally of both ego and superego, is thus in the verbal dream "Autodidasker" representative, specifically of the apposition—i.e., the coincidence topographically—of "ideal ego" and ego ideal.

*

The dream speech has been characterized in the foregoing as direct speech, either owning or lacking motor or sensory qualities in the hallucinatory experience of the dreamer. It is a day residue and it may be a product of dream work but it originates and exists independently from the rest of the dream. Its occurrence depends upon the temporary re-establishment of the dreamer's superego beside his ego with the result that the speech is representative simultaneously of both of these institutions. The hallucinatory particularities of the "spoken word" are as variable as is its place in the manifest content: speech may but need not be either spoken or heard, wholly or mainly so, it may be traceable to a vocabulary or neologistic, part

[33] Freud, *New Introductory Lectures to Psychoanalysis* (Chap. XXI). W. W. Norton, New York, 1933.

[34] This term, although first employed by Freud for the superego, was subsequently discarded and is therefore free for the employment suggested above.

of a dialogue or a soliloquy and it may issue from the dreamer, from someone else, or from no one.

This precludes a selective identification of speech-motor or auditory hallucination in the dream as effects of ego or superego respectively, and suggests instead that one remember the general dependence of speaking and hearing upon one another as exemplified in the deaf and as experimentally studied. Speech cannot, obviously, be heard unless it is spoken; but neither can it be spoken without being heard. If it is, it becomes uncontrolled; it gains volume, loses inflection and grows defective in enunciation.[35] Auditory self-observation proves thus requisite to speech-motor performance in a manner akin to that in which other motor performance is dependent upon "semicircular" self-observation. One cannot, in other words, achieve proper co-ordination in either action or speech without the assistance of a perceptive and, at the same time, corrective sensory apparatus genetically connected with the superego.[36]

This observation, belonging to the analysis of perception, cannot explain the presence, absence or prevalence of hallucination of one or the other phase of speech in a dream. Nor can metapsychology do so at present. "It is most probable," Freud wrote as late as 1932,[37] in discussing the "anatomy of the mental personality," "that the degree of these (topographical) differentiations is very variable in different individuals and it is possible that, in functioning,

[35] Wiener, Norbert, The Human Use of Human Beings. Houghton Mifflin Co., Boston, 1950.

[36] Isakower, who elaborates upon the genetic connection of the organ of equilibrium and the auditory sphere as the nucleus of the superego does not, however, refer to the dependence, indispensable to a theory of the spoken word in the dream, of speech motility upon auditory perception. ("On the Exceptional Position of the Auditory Sphere," Int. J. Psa., XX, 1939, p. 340.)

[37] Neue Folge der Vorlesungen zur Einführung in die Psychoanalyse. Int. Psa. Verlag, Wien, p. 111. Translated by the present writer.

they are altered, and become subject to a temporary in-volution." In the case of the dream speech, it is instead of an "involution" a temporary differentiation, whose de-gree as well as whose relation to the depth of sleep, i.e., to a relative wakefulness of the dreamer, is unknown. It remains therefore ununderstood why, e.g., the verbal dream combines as it appears to do, lack of motor and sensory qualities with proximity to arousal. An "alteration in functioning," i.e., in precipitating the spoken word, is likewise, extant; it shall be shown to consist in a topo-graphical modification concerning the delimitative char-acteristics of ego and superego and to contribute toward the explanation of the aforementioned ambiguity of the spoken word.

The study of hallucination of speech in the dream is thus reduced to a study of its *production*. A theory of the spoken word, based upon the re-establishment in the dreamer of his superego, must supply the economy and the dynamics of this topographical process. It is toward both these pur-poses that one has to apply observations of phenomena other than dreams. For the study of the economy it is convenient to draw upon reports of speech-motor and auditory experiences in the aphasic, the normal and the schizophrenic; for an investigation of the dynamics it is necessary to supplement Freud's fundamental study on the role of the superego in humor.

Isakower,[38] in order to show that the economy prevalent during auditory hallucination is one of crisis, has referred instructively to a certain self-observation of Freud's pub-lished in his study on "Aphasia." A more comprehensive quotation of the passage is even more instructive. Freud,[39] discussing observations of Huglings Jackson, in order to

[38] *Op. cit.*, p. 347.
[39] *Zur Auffassung der Aphasie*. Deuticke, Leipzig und Wien, 1891.

show that speech remainders in motor aphasia may exceed
"yes" and "no" and certain powerful curses (sacré nom de
Dieu, Goddam, etc.), quotes two instances which "permit,"
as he expresses it, "a very plausible interpretation. A man
. . . . who could only say 'I want protection' owed his
aphasia to a brawl in which, after being struck on the head,
he had lost consciousness and collapsed. And a second one
who had the strange speech remainder 'List complete' was
a clerk whom the condition had struck down after the
strenuous work of completing a catalogue. Such examples
suggest that these speech remainders are the last words
produced by the speech apparatus before the onset of its
morbid condition *perhaps already under the influence of
the very beginning of its realization*"[40] (*. . . . vielleicht
bereits in Ahnung derselben*). "I would explain," Freud
goes on to say, "the persistence of this last modification
with its intensity, provided that it takes place at a moment
of great internal excitement" (*Ich möchte das Verbleiben
dieser letzten Modifikation aus deren Intensität erklären,
wenn sie im Momente einer grossen inneren Erregung er-
folgt.*) Perhaps better translated more freely: If this last
modification of speech through the aphasic process occurs
at a moment of great inner excitement its very intensity
should serve as an explanation for its persistence. "I remember," Freud concludes, adding a self-observation,
"that I have twice felt myself in danger of my life and
each time the perception came quite suddenly. In both
cases I thought to myself, 'Now it's all up with you,' and,
although my internal speech is as a rule carried on with
quite indistinct sound images and only faint sensations in
the lips, yet in the moment of danger I heard these words
as though someone were shouting them in my ear and saw

40 *Italics mine.*

them at the same time as though they were printed on a fluttering piece of paper."

Isakower, who confines himself to this last example, follows it with the comment: "The superego character of these words is to be remarked, which sound like the pronouncement of judgment by a powerful authority, while at the same time the verdict can be read. . . . One could also conceive of the externalization as being the result of a narrowing of the personality to the body-ego as a consequence of the shock." And he precedes it with an observation of his own: "A 26-year-old schizophrenic (without epilepsy) in whom impoverishment and blunting of the inner life dominated the scene . . . . complained of attacks of physical incapacity to work, so that he had to lay aside whatever he held in his hands, and he also felt a heavy pressure down upon the top of his head. . . . At the same time something else always happened which the patient called 'self-talking' *(Selbstredung);* he was obliged to repeat aloud over and over: 'I am Max Koch from Alland' (which in fact he was). In a critical situation, when a threatened disruption of the ego was, as it were, acutely experienced, being condensed into a moment, this ego affirmed its existence by a magic formula, which can easily be understood as a faithful reproduction of what had been instilled into him as a child." This, in turn, is preceded by another comment upon Freud's well-known interpretation of the delusions of observation: "The hallucinatory voices serve the purpose, among other things, of warning the sick person of the danger of being overpowered by the id. When the integrity of the personality is threatened from within, the superego reveals both its history and its genesis; that is, it reveals not only the way in which its nucleus arose but also of what its nucleus consists."[41]

[41] Cf. Freud, (1914), "On Narcissism: An Introduction." *Collected Papers,* IV, p. 53. London: Hogarth Press, 1925. (Continued on p. 150.)

The exigency prevailing in all of these observations is caused by the imminence of destruction: through a blow on the head, through the unknown aphasic or schizophrenic process, through an accident that promises to be fatal. The economy is, therefore, in all of them, one of crisis; the topography one of disintegration of ego. But the ego disintegrates, as Freud has exemplified with the splitting up of a crystal, along the lines structural to its integration. Ego and superego, regressing under the impact of trauma, break apart; and aware of the impact communicate with each other as the (in part "prehistoric") child and the (in part "archaic") parent out of whom they originally developed. The resultant speech has the characteristics, sensory and topographical, of the dream speech. "I want protection" is a spoken demand of the infantile ego upon the parental superego; "List complete" is a spoken ambiguity, expressive of a pleading by the ego concerning a job well done and of a reassuring by the superego through commendation; it is traceable to either one of these institutions. "Now it is all up with you" is more heard (and seen) than spoken and shouted by a "someone," the re-externalized superego (—model), into the "ears," part of the (body-) ego. "I am Max Koch from Alland," finally, is an instance of the prevalence of the motor component; yet its designation as *Selbstredung* intimates that the experience is one of being made to speak, beside speaking. It is this last speech that bears the closest resemblance to

---

"For that which prompted the person to form an ego-ideal, over which his conscience keeps guard, was the influence of parental criticism (conveyed to him by the medium of the voice), reinforced, as time went on, by those who trained and taught the child and by all the other persons of his environment—an indefinite host, too numerous to reckon (fellow-men, public opinion) . . . The voices, as well as the indefinite number of speakers, are brought into the foreground again by the disease, and so the evolution of conscience is regressively reproduced."

the incipient delusions of observation, where the observers
affirm; and their speech is, at first, not critical but assertive. It verbalizes, although in projection, from the standpoint of the superego: identity; and from that of the ego:
existence.[42]

None of these speeches is understandable without the
economic emergency and its realization. The latter,
precipitative of "involution" (historic regression) and "alteration" (topographical redifferentiation) opposes ego
and superego and is productive of speech.

I suggest that the economy here described be considered
the economy of the dream speech. No other hypothesis
justifies adding the production of direct speech as a third
instance of re-establishment of the superego in the dreamer
to the two described previously by Freud. Such temporary
re-establishment occurs, he wrote, as a "reaction against
the dream" (*Einschreiten gegen den Traum*), in particular "in response to the stimulation (of the superego)
by the unconscious wish-fulfilment."[43] We may complement: it occurs in response to a threat to the ego organization of the dreamer in the course of the wish fulfillment.
One could say of both aspects that they present the superego as reinforcing, reintegratively, the economically insufficient dream censor; and that the first places the accent
upon an intolerant superego imposing itself upon the ego
while the second emphasizes the need for support of an
ego invoking the superego for its protection.[44] Freud's ob-

[42] Cf., e.g., Freud's own example: "Now she is thinking of it again" and
"Now he is going away" (*loc. cit.*).

[43] "Remarks Upon the Theory and Practice of Dream-Interpretation,"
loc. cit.

[44] Shakespeare, in *Richard III* (I, iv.) has presented a variant: a
"punishment dream" containing "direct speech." Here, of course, there is
no superego imposing itself upon an ego invoking it for its protection; but
the two are involved, instead, in the sadomasochistic relation formulated
by Freud. (Cf. quotation and reference on pp. 134 f.) There are, consequently, *two* speeches: one spoken by a representative of the parent (super-

servation of the schizophrenic treatment by the dreamer of word remainders does not, to say the least, contravene this hypothesis; it is in consequence of the same economy that the dream, ordinarily a mere "model of the psychotic state," produces, upon occasion, phenomena pathognomonic for a psychotic disturbance.

Considerations that have no place in the present context suggest that the particular censorial function, that is defective and thereby contributory to the economical crisis productive of direct speech in the dream, is the suppression of affect.

*

If the superego is temporarily re-established, it must be endowed with substantial quantities of narcissistic cathexis. In the sleeper these quantities are withdrawn into the id, in the dreamer they are in part released to the ego; in the production of direct speech an excess of them becomes available for the development of the censor into as much of a superego as is compatible with the state of sleep.

The displacement of great quantities of cathexis upon the superego as a means of "the ego's . . . assertion of its . . . . invulnerability" at the price of an illusion has been

---

ego) and the second by one of the dreamer (ego) ; the former threatening punishment and the latter invoking it. Clarence, the dreamer, meets his father-in-law and his cousin in Hades:

Clarence: The first that there did greet my stranger soul,
Was my great father-in-law, renowned Warwick;
Who cried aloud, '*What scourge for perjury*
Can this dark monarchy afford false Clarence?'
And so he vanished: then came wandering by
A shadow like an angel, with bright hair
Dabbled in blood; and he shriek'd out loud,
'*Clarence is come,—false, fleeting, perjur'd Clarence,*
That stabb'd me in the field by Tewksbury;—
Seize on him! Furies, take him unto torment.'

Yet at the moment of trauma, when the murderer sees his dead victim "dabbled in blood," ego and superego join in affirming, self-observatively, identity and existence. "*Clarence is come*" is the equivalent of the aforementioned auditory hallucination in the incipient delusion of observation.

described by Freud in his investigation of humor.[45] His study, exhaustive and yet at the same time incomplete, permits a supplementation illustrable with his own example of the condemned man who, on his way to the gallows on Monday, says: "Na die Woche fängt gut an!"[46] This from the mouth of the criminal, is, as Freud has observed, expressive of an illusion; the week actually could not have started worse. However, were it said by the hangman, it would be descriptive of a reality; it is for him that the week could not actually have started better. He has a customer on the very first day, earns a fee, indulges in his profession and, last but not least, is entitled to call the week a week because he will still be alive at its end. The condemned man, in other words, speaks as hangman; and the illusion is the reality under conditions of an identification. The latter, as illustrated by the time and place of the anecdote, (19th century Vienna, where only homicide brought about execution) is an identification of one murderer with another; the first a criminal to be punished, the second an executive of the law, inflicting the punishment as prescribed by the *ius talionis*. The relation between them is that between ego and superego in the case of the punishment dream as described by Freud. The identification, however, prerequisite to the humorous elaboration is describable, interpersonally, as one of the "prehistoric" child with the "archaic" parent and, intrapersonally, as one of the earliest with the later subject of the same strivings; in other words, if the term suggested above be accepted, of the ideal ego with the ego ideal.

The humorous speech is one normal production, the dream speech is another. Both depend upon the displacement of great quantities of narcissistic cathexis from the ego upon the superego, effecting an approximation of

45 (1928), "Humor," *Collected Papers*, V. Hogarth Press, London, 1950.
46 Approximation: "This week's off to a good start . . . !"

parts of these institutions. The cathectic process, precipitated by a crisis in the psychic economy of the dreamer, may of course dynamically be of the nature of an oscillation. Topographically it has led, at the time of the speech, to a juxtaposition between the subject of an unconscious infantile dream wish and that of the (likewise instinctual) forces compelling its inhibition or modification. The effect is either a fusion of the two subjects or their opposition at closest range; in most instances perhaps both. Speech can therefore be produced as well as suppressed. (The dream speech contributed by Hugh-Hellmuth in the famous "Dream of the *Liebesdienste*" shows the two alternating, because the suppression, incomplete as it is, has here merely reduced the production to that of an "understandable murmur.")

The suggestion initiating the present investigation, which had the superego contribute direct speech to the dream, has proven inaccurate. The "spoken word" is produced jointly by ego and superego, irrespective of motor or sensory qualities in a given dream. The thought conveyed by the speech is ambiguous; for it is expressive of both of these institutions and traceable to the second phase of the formation of dream, where the two are still differentiated and capable of contributing jointly. The speech proper, i.e., the verbalization, belongs to the third phase. Its dynamics are an abrupt displacement of cathectic quantities in consequence of an economic crisis, precipitative of a transient re-establishment of the superego in the dreamer. (The particular nature of this crisis and the relation, dependent upon it, of the dream speech to the rest of the manifest content could not be dealt with in the framework of the present communication.) The topography of the "spoken word" is that of an approximation of ego and superego, in particular: ideal ego and ego ideal—

an instance of "involution" (through incomplete reintegration) and "alteration" of their "delimitative characteristics in the course of their functioning," such as has been suggested by Freud.

Ego and superego join, in other words, twice: once in producing the thought while they exist *as yet* and, schematically speaking, before the dream is dreamed; and the other time in producing the verbalization while they exist *again* and the speech occurs in the dream.

Since the relation of ego and superego, although intra-personal, has interpersonal characteristics their topographical approximation may lead to their *ap*position or *op*position. The thought issued jointly may therefore be ambiguous or antithetic; its verbalization produced or suppressed. Speech can thus enter the dream, be eliminated from it, verbalized or attenuated to vocalization.

Both the thought expressed by the speech and the speech itself are subjectable to all phases of dream-work. It is in the second of these two instances that the word images of the speech are the object of the "distortion" with the result that the speech may become neologistic. Such a "schizophrenic" complexion of the spoken word in the dream supports the suggestion, once made by Freud, that word images be considered as nuclear to the ego. For the dreamer's ego is known to approximate that of the psychotic.

Part Six

REVIEWER'S OPINION ON CONTROVERSIAL QUESTIONS

FREUD'S WRITINGS ON THE DREAM

1899 Eine erfüllte Traumahnung (A Dream Prophecy Fulfilled). *Gesammelte Werke*, XVII. Imago Publishing Co., London.

1900 *The Interpretation of Dreams.* Macmillan, New York, 1913.

1901 *On the Dream.* W. W. Norton, New York, 1952.

1912 The Employment of Dream-Interpretation in Psycho-Analysis. *Collected Papers*, II. Hogarth Press, London, 1924.

1913 The Occurrence in Dreams of Material from Fairy-Tales. *Collected Papers*, IV.
A Dream which Bore Testimony. *Collected Papers*, II.

1916 Metapsychological Supplement to the Theory of Dreams. *Collected Papers*, IV.

1917 The Dream. Chapter II in *A General Introduction to Psychoanalysis*. Boni and Liveright, New York.

1922 Dreams and Telepathy. *Collected Papers*, IV.

1923 Remarks upon the Theory and Practice of Dream-Interpretation. *Collected Papers*, V.
Josef Popper-Lynkeus und die Theorie des Traumes (Josef Popper-Lynkeus and the Theory of the Dream). *Gesammelte Werke*, XIII.

1925 Some Additional Notes upon Dream-Interpretation as a Whole. *Collected Papers*, V.

1929 Brief an Maxim Leroy über einen Traum des Cartesius (Letter to Maxim Leroy on a Dream of Descartes). *Gesammelte Werke*, XIV.

1933 Revision of the Theory of the Dream (Chap. XXIX), Dreams and the Occult (Chap. XXX), *New Introductory Lectures to Psychoanalysis*. W. W. Norton, New York, 1933.

1938 Dream Interpretation as an Illustration (Chap. V), *An Outline of Psychoanalysis*. W. W. Norton, New York, 1949.

INDEX

Dream (*Continued*)
  "spoken word" in, 128-155
  "telepathic," 36-37
  the "negative" in, 75-77
  transformation of thoughts into
      pictures, 30, 31, 75-77, 126
  traumatic, 79
  traumatic genesis of, 77-81
  typical, 15, 24-31, 64
  unpleasant nature of, 78
  upon dental stimulation, 14-24
  "verbal," 139, 143
  wish fulfillment in, 18, 29, 38, 59,
      78-79, 135-137, 151
  writing down of, 115-116
  see also Anxiety-, Arousal-, Blank-,
      Examination-, Mirror-, Pun-
      ishment-Dream, *and* Night-
      mare
Dream analysis
  among Indians, 63-64
  and resistance, 112, 115
  method of, 118-127
Dream Doctors, 62
Dream hallucinations, 56-57
Dream material
  and day residue, 140
  and reading matter, 130, 139
  and thoughts, 49
  distinguished from dream work,
      83, 125-126
Dream screen, 110-118
Dream speech
  alteration, 137-138
  ambiguity, 142-143, 147
  compared to waking speech, 140
  described by dreamer, 138-139
  economy of, 151
  elements of, 140
  fragmentation in, 137-138
  meaningless, 140
  production of, 147-155
  selection, 137-138
  sensory character of, 138-139
  spoken or heard vs. read, 139
  see also Dream, spoken word in
Dream Theory, nature of addenda
      and emendations, 72-73, 126-127
Dream work, 18, 48, 60, 74, 80, 83,
      98, 125, 131-132, 141-143, 155
  and aggression, 57, 94
  and plastic representation, 141-143

Economo, 107
Ego, 83, 85, 133
  analysis of, 91, 115-118
  and boredom, 100-103
  and dream speech, 133-155
  and fantasies, 142-143
  and humor, 152-154
  and id-libido, 86-88
  and motor qualities of speech,
      138-139
  and repression, 137
  and schizophrenia, 149
  and sleep, 53-56, 84-87, 89-90, 95
  and word images, 155
  boundary, 89
  cathectic alterations of, 86-87, 88,
      90-91
  cognitive function of, 97, 106
  disintegration of, 149-151
  dissociation of functions of, 86
  failure of synthetic function of,
      107
  in dream and hypnosis, 34-35
  in dreaming, 87-94
  in falling asleep, 84-87, 89-90
  in waking up, 95-103
  narcissistic cathexis of, 104-105
  redifferentiation of, 86
  restitution of, 107
Ego feeling
  in dream, 21-24, 87-91, 100
  in sleep, 104
  loss of, 104-105
Ego ideal, 135, 143-145, 150
  and ideal ego, 145, 153-155
  see also Superego
Ehrenwald, J., 38-43
Eisenbud, J., 36-37
Eisenstein, V. W., 69-70
Eisler, R., 56
Eissler, K. R., 91, 115-118
Eissler, R. S., 91, 115-118
Ellis, A., 36-37
Empathy, 125
Entfremdung
  see Estrangement
Enuresis
  and sleep disturbances, 54
Epilepsy, 149
Epileptic attacks, and sleep, 55-57
Erotogeneity, 67
Erythrophobia, 117

Semantics, 106
Shakespeare, W., 151-152
Silberer, H., 98, 104, 113
Simmel, E., 52-58, 84
Skin symptoms, 114
Sleep
  and aggression, 56-57
  and attention to outside stimuli,
    97
  and "basic" dream, 126
  and death, 59, 105, 108
  and dream screen, 110-115
  and masturbation, 54, 56, 84
  and schizophrenia, 105, 155
  and sense of time, 107
  as physiological problem, 90, 126
  as return to womb, 112
  bioanalysis of, 103-109
  disturbances of, 49-58, 84-87
  dreamless, 55, 89-90, 103-110
  motor-cathexis in, 34-35, 53-54, 56
  nature of, 95-96, 103-109, 126
  psychopathology of falling asleep,
    84-87, 89-90
  wish to, 108-109, 111
  see also Hypersomnia, Insomnia,
    and Awakening
Sleep phobia, 52, 53-54, 84
Sleep rituals, 54
Somatic compliance, 52
Somnambulism, 56
Sprott, W. J. H., 80
Steckel, W., 74
Sterba, R., 31-32
Stereotypy, 117
Stuttering, 65
Sublimation, 145
Suicide, 114
Superego, 83, 94, 106
  and censor, 98, 136
  and dream, 134-155
  and ego, 133-155
  and humor, 147
  and masturbation, 54, 84
  auditory nucleus of, 128, 133, 146
  contribution of to dream, 128-155
  narcissistic cathexis of, 152-155
  origin of, 133-134
  representation of in dream, 82
Symbols
  choice of, 14
  functional, 98

Symbols (*Continued*)
  function of, 113
  translation of, 120, 123
  unconscious understanding of, 16
Symbolic action, 13, 37
Symbolism
  and hypnosis, 16, 33
  compared to allegory and meta-
    phor, 124
  experimental study of, 16
  discussion of term, 13
  functional, 98
  in dreams, 13-24
  of knife, 39
  of losing teeth, 14-24
Symbolization, 15, 80, 119
Symptomatic action, 37

Tagesgedanken, unerledigte, 122
Tarachow, S., 69
Tendency (Alexander & Wilson), 67
Thought
  and dream work, 126, 132-133
  compulsive, 140-141
  representation of in dreams, 75-
    77, 98-99
  unfinished, 122
Tiefenperson, 90
Toffelmier, G., 62
Transference, and dream, 31-32, 39,
    44-46, 60, 91-94, 113, 143
Traumatic neurosis, 77-78
Traumatic situations, reproduction
    of, 77-79, 92-93
Triebdurchbruch, 93
Twilight states, 55-56

Ulcer, 67

Vector (Alexander & Wilson), 67

Waelder, R., 128, 137
Weltuntergangserlebnis, 87
Wiener, N., 146
Wilson, G. W., 66-68
Windholz, E., 52-58
Wisdom, J. O., 79-81, 121
Word images
  "schizophrenic" treatment of, 143-
    145
  and ego, 155
Wotte, H., 13-14

Zulliger, H., 37-38